Protecting Whitney

THE MEMOIR OF HER BODYGUARD

DAVID ROBERTS

CHICAGO
REVIEW
PRESS

Library of Congress Cataloging-in-Publication Data
Names: Roberts, David (Bodyguard) author.
Title: Protecting Whitney : the memoir of her bodyguard / David Roberts.
Description: Chicago : Chicago Review Press, 2025. | Summary: "David
Roberts was hired in 1988 to provide security for the UK portion of Whitney
Houston's Moment of Truth world tour. Accustomed to working for diplomats
and Fortune 500 clients, Roberts had reservations about working with a pop
star. But from the moment they met at Heathrow Airport, Houston's heart of
gold won him over. Roberts would work for Houston for seven years as her
career soared to its pinnacle. His memoir reveals heartwarming anecdotes of
life with one of the world's most recognizable stars, including privately shared
moments such as the birth of Whitney's daughter, Bobbi Kristina. But there
are also shocking and heartbreaking revelations, as Roberts was present for
some of Houston's most challenging ordeals. His heart was ultimately shattered
as he witnessed her succumb to the one threat he could not protect her from:
herself"— Provided by publisher.
Identifiers: LCCN 2024034264 (print) | LCCN 2024034265 (ebook) | ISBN
9780914090373 (hardcover) | ISBN 9780914090427 (adobe pdf) | ISBN
9780914090458 (epub)
Subjects: LCSH: Roberts, David (Bodyguard) | Houston, Whitney. |
Bodyguards—Biography. | LCGFT: Autobiographies.
Classification: LCC ML429.R59 A3 2025 (print) | LCC ML429.R59 (ebook) |
DDC 363.28/9092 [B]—dc23/eng/20240801
LC record available at https://lccn.loc.gov/2024034264
LC ebook record available at https://lccn.loc.gov/2024034265

The author gratefully acknowledges the writing assistance of Katy Van Sant

Typesetting: Jonathan Hahn

Printed in the United States of America
5 4 3 2 1

To my dearest friend, brother, confidant, and mentor
Gene "Popeye" Botel
"Too many have died before their time—
just not the right ones!"

If you or someone you know is struggling with addiction, depression, or any other emotional challenge, Crisis Text Line is here to support you. Simply text HOME to 741741 to reach a volunteer crisis counselor—24/7, free, confidential.

Contents

Preface

After spending so many years in angry contemplation, I found it cathartic to finally recall, relive, and recount my experiences, my life, as Whitney Houston's bodyguard. I am hoping that by sharing this story, you can get to know her more deeply and appreciate what we lost from this world when she died.

I will start by answering the questions I am often asked:

Yes, I was Whitney Houston's bodyguard.

No, I am not Kevin Costner. He's taller.

Was real life with her like it was in the movie? Is life ever like it is in the movies? Sometimes yes and sometimes no.

Did I love her? Yes, but perhaps not in the way you are thinking. Show me someone who didn't.

Did I ever take a bullet for her? Again, perhaps not in the way you are thinking. But I've realized all these many years later that, yes, I really did.

I saw that bullet coming and knew that if I stepped up to stop it, I would be hit, and it would be one of the most painful experiences of my life. I also knew that I had no choice. I saw it speeding toward that beautiful and talented woman, I knew it could kill her, and I had to step in front of it to try to save her, no matter the cost to me. That was my promise to her: to protect her, no matter what.

So I took that bullet—I shone a light on the destructive forces that were taking away her voice, her happiness, and her life. The price I paid for that choice was immense, but I have no regrets. I still have the scar; it is on my heart and was reopened on the day she died. You will see it when you read the story that follows.

Some names of individuals and identifying details mentioned in this book have been fictionalized. The fictional names are indicated by SMALL CAPS on first mention. Any similarity between the fictionalized names and the names of real people is strictly coincidental.

INTRODUCTION
Grand Canyon, March 1995

"If she doesn't stop, she'll never sing again."

As the concerned, gray-bearded doctor sitting across from me explained the damage to Whitney's vocal cords, I stared out the window of the Cessna at crimson cliffs and towering spires. The plane dipped down into the Grand Canyon, a massive gouge in the desert reaching down to a twisting, green liquid thread—so far from the misty mountains and curling coves of my home in rural coastal Wales, and yet similar in the majesty and purity of the landscape.

Dr. Julian Groff, Whitney's throat doctor, had flown out from Miami to Arizona the day before to examine her. He then put out a call asking that I meet him the next day to go up in a plane and fly over the canyon for a couple of hours. It was an offer I didn't want to refuse, and knowing Whitney would definitely not be going anywhere that day, I agreed. The views were outstanding, beyond anything I imagined, and truly worthy of wonder-of-the-world status, but the news and prognosis he had to impart over the hum of the engine brought me back to earth.

The anger in me began to rise. I thought of that magnificent, exquisite voice that could reach into one's heart and soul with its range

1

and depth—now in danger of being lost forever. I was furious at all those who facilitated Whitney's ability to do this to herself, who looked the other way because they saw her voice box as a cash machine. As her protection officer, it was my responsibility to keep her safe at all costs. And yet the good doctor was asking me to address a threat I had not been trained to handle. A bomb or sniper's bullet could be avoided, deferred, or mitigated with accurate situational assessments. But this significantly more insidious threat, the terrorist that lurks within, was the most daunting.

As shock and ire gave way to resignation and resolve to do what had to be done, I was curious about one thing in particular . . .

"Doc, why are you telling *me* this?"

Looking at me pointedly, he said, "Because you're the only one I can speak to with sufficient common sense to get something done."

What an awesome responsibility he had just laid firmly on my shoulders. He was not speaking to her husband, her manager, her father, her mother, or anyone else who would normally be expected to look out for her voice or her career. Just her bodyguard.

1

Pop-Star Protection

In February 1988, Bob O'Brien of the US Embassy in London called me at my company, Churchill Security Consultancy. He wanted me to deploy on an executive protection assignment for a US citizen coming to the UK. Over the years I had developed a good professional working relationship with Bob, who would frequently call and ask me to look after heads of US corporations traveling to the UK and Europe. I assumed this was a typical wealthy US client, a diplomat or Fortune 500 CEO with requirements to travel through Europe, for whom I'd provide active threat assessment and personal security protection.

However, Bob wanted to know if I would consider looking after Whitney Houston.

I immediately inquired, "Who's he?"

Bob explained that she was a woman and a singer. I asked if she sang opera, still operating on the basis of the type of clients I was used to. Other than Motown, soul, and jazz, with a special penchant for saxophonist Kenny G, my main love was Welsh choral music. When Bob told me that Houston was a global pop icon, I responded with trepidation. "Sorry, Bob, but I don't do sex, drugs, and rock 'n' roll."

"Too late, my friend," he said. He'd already thrown my name into the hat and was counting on me to do my thing. He had scheduled an interview for me with Wallace LaPrade, the former head of the New York office of the FBI. I obliged and agreed to attend the meeting.

As a private close protection (CP) officer—colloquially known as a bodyguard—clients may have thought they were interviewing me for suitability for the role, but in reality, I was interviewing them to determine whether I would be willing to die for the "principal"—the person I was charged to protect. The mere thought of looking after a pop star did not inspire me to anticipate a successful outcome for the interview.

I called my teenage daughter, Sara, and asked her if she had ever heard of this Whitney Houston person.

"Oh, Dad," she responded, "I want to dance with somebody!"

I told her she could dance all she liked after she answered my question as to who this woman was. Sara provided her teenage insight on the relatively new musical phenomenon that reportedly was Whitney Houston.

Intrigued, and instinctively undertaking my usual potential client homework, I went to the Edgware music store and found out this woman had already produced two albums. I bought both her CDs, brought them back to my office, and played them. I was more than impressed. She was captivating, her voice golden. I thought to myself, *This woman can sing.*

I headed to the interview with former agent in charge LaPrade at the Dorchester Hotel. LaPrade had been commissioned by an organization known as Nippy Inc., Houston's corporation, and was charged with traveling abroad to hire security for Houston's forthcoming European tour. Her voice and the photographs on the covers of both albums led me to believe Whitney Houston just might prove to be someone worth taking a bullet for. However, based on frequent dealings with musicians at Camden Town Market, as well as stars at Wembley during my police officer years, I remained extremely skeptical. This was still the world of international rock 'n' roll, against which I held an extremely negative bias.

Although I left the force in 1984 to start my own business, I will always be a policeman at heart. My father was the chief inspector of police for North Wales, and I followed him into the North Wales Police after serving in the Royal Air Force Police, where I was initially posted in Northern Ireland and experienced much of the Troubles firsthand. Based on my military experience, I trained to be a sniper with the newly formed firearms department of the North Wales Police, then transferred to the Metropolitan Police in London in 1977, also serving as a sniper. Two years later I was promoted to sergeant and served at Harrow Road, where I was stabbed by a suspect who remains "wanted on warrant" for my attempted murder. Then it was on to the Special Patrol Group—at that time the predominant crime-catchers of the Metropolitan Police—before moving to the Royalty & Diplomatic Protection Department of the Met at New Scotland Yard, whose expert executive protection training was based on the cutting-edge protocols and doctrines of the Special Air Service.

At the time of my resignation, I was the only "former police" specialist trained in the discipline of close personal protection operating in the private sector with that level of training. As a law enforcement sniper, I'd been deployed at the 1980 Iranian Embassy siege, and in the ongoing fight against terrorism was involved in the immediate response to the December 1983 IRA bombing of Harrods in London. I learned from these experiences, as well as from my participation in those of a more celebratory sort, such as the marriage of Prince Charles and Lady Di, and Pope John Paul II's 1982 visit to London. Consequently, my business was quite successful.

Not particularly wanting or needing this pop-star gig, I played up the part of the quintessential arrogant Brit during my interview with LaPrade. I categorically refused, probably in a more demeaning tone than intended, his demands for teams of snipers and bomb dogs for every venue, none of which was even remotely possible on the streets of the UK anyway, and certainly not for a pop singer, which is precisely what I told him. "It's not going to happen, sir," was my refrain throughout the interview.

I concluded the meeting by assuring the gentleman I would charge significantly more than any other person or company he intended to interview while in locus. He nevertheless thanked me, and I departed feeling sure I would not be considered for the assignment but had discharged my professional obligations to Bob O'Brien.

Bob's next call, a few weeks later, knocked me sideways. To my shock and horror, I had been awarded the contract to represent Whitney Houston on the British leg of her tour.

On April 8, 1988, I was with my wife in Paris celebrating her fortieth birthday when I received a call to inform me that Ms. Houston, my future principal, would be arriving at Heathrow on the Concorde the very next day. I would come to learn that this last-minute, knee-jerk, ill-prepared planning and arrangement was typical of how the entire Nippy Inc. operation worked. I returned to London immediately and met Larry Wansley, the security director for Whitney's European tour. A strong Black man with the most pleasant and unruffled demeanor you could imagine, Larry was a former undercover FBI agent and the director of security for the Dallas Cowboys. He was taking a sabbatical during the off-season to work for Whitney. He was ten years my senior, with no special training in the disciplines of executive protection, but with an abundance of common sense that had kept him alive in some very precarious situations.

Larry appeared to recognize in me the potential for professional synergy, as I could furnish him the vital element he needed: local knowledge and associated expertise in the UK. He too was often bemused by the lack of organization of the representing corporation, and sought to cover the failings by stating, "David, the beat goes on." I took it to mean that no matter what Whitney's people do, how unpredictable and ill-advised it may be, we just carry on with our task the best we can. That became our standard salutation and continues to this very day, four decades later.

As we made the drive to Heathrow to meet her plane, Larry gave me the rundown on Whitney's entourage and executive party. He explained to me that many of its members were not hired because of a specific skill, but rather because they were Whitney's friends and family, and she always looked after her own. Some were just there to party. Others were desperate to stay in Whitney's good graces to keep their livelihoods. This created an unpredictable environment, always a hindrance to good security.

When she appeared via the airport's VIP exit and Larry did the introductions, I found my rock 'n' roll preconceptions pleasantly contradicted in her specific regard. She struck me right away as gracious, actually somewhat shy and introverted, and ever so well-mannered— not to mention one of the most beautiful women I had ever met.

"You're terribly English, David," she said when I greeted her and offered my hand to shake formally.

"Actually, I'm Welsh," I replied. Like many Welshmen, I tend to wear my heart on my sleeve, so I put that out there immediately. We chatted about Wales, and I found her to be very well informed. Many, if not most, Americans do not know where Wales is or even that it is a part of the UK.

It was subsequently remarkable to me that whenever we were in the company of Whitney's group, and until I learned the particulars of their vernacular, she proceeded to "translate" her entourage's expletive-riddled Newark slang. She would turn to me and translate, effectively in a style of Queen's English, precisely what was being said, which was received with a sense of amusement by those present. In those days I smoked, and on one occasion announced to the group, in local London slang and without thinking, that I was "just going outside to have a blow on a fag."

While my intentions would have been obvious to Londoners, in American English these words had an entirely different and shocking connotation. The laughter was raucous and had them rolling on the floor. When most had picked themselves up and were able to talk and explain, I realized why (and not without some embarrassment). But we all had a good laugh over it.

———————

Larry briefed me on the plethora of security threats we were to address. There were scores of potentially deadly stalkers and crazies worldwide, including several then at large in the UK, the most worrying of whom seemed to be a man of former military experience based in Wolverhampton. He had reportedly "planned to take Whitney and their children to heaven." My worries were intensified for the Birmingham leg of the tour.

In addition, there was another crazy, this one from Yorkshire, who appeared to have the means and desire to travel to New Jersey to carry out his evil threats on Whitney there. He was also troubled by an obsession with the actress Victoria Principal, creating mayhem for her and her staff as well. I rang up Inspector Briar at the Wheatfield police station to make sure this threat to my principal was contained and controlled for our movements in the UK.

The more I learned, the more I knew keeping Whitney safe was going to be a truly monumental challenge, unlike anything I'd experienced looking after CEOs or diplomats. With Ms. Houston and her entourage, I sensed there was no alternative but for me to take a hands-on approach from start to finish. Our overall corporate reputation at Churchill would rely upon it. Larry agreed to supply me with additional support staff. However, I could not risk leaving this solely in their hands. There was never any chance that I would not be directly involved 24/7 for the duration of the UK tour.

With Whitney's powder-blue Rolls-Royce in the lead, the convoy headed to the private house that had been rented for the London phase of the tour, rather than a hotel; someone had suggested the private residence arrangement to be more discreet and secure. My business partner at Churchill, JOHN KINGSLEY, had only been able to execute a rush security check on the premises due to the last-minute communication of the arrival. He was deeply concerned, and with a résumé like his it was always wise to listen. For decades Kingsley had worked for a covert arm of British intelligence, one that remains a closely guarded secret even today. Wiry, tough, and highly skilled, he liked to annoyingly slurp his tea, smoke incessantly, and act the "gray man"—the one no one ever notices in a crowd. In short, he was the master of clandestine operations.

Kingsley's concerns were twofold. First, the house was nowhere near secure enough for a client of Whitney's profile. Second, it had little perimeter wall or fencing to speak of, not even much of a screen of trees, which is crucial to block the long lenses of the paparazzi. Kingsley was also deeply suspicious of the motives of the person renting the house. An opportunity to sell covertly obtained photos or overheard conversations to the media could be quite lucrative. Even as he and the team had been sweeping the place for bugging devices and cameras, or any drugs that may have been planted there, the owner showed up and tried to gain access. Though the owner and his agent objected most vociferously, Kingsley didn't give a damn and most rigorously denied them. Suspicions aroused, Kingsley undertook a series of deep background checks. It turned out the owner was a Wall Street banker who had recently lost a fortune in dealings on the stock exchange. In Kingsley's professional opinion, anyone desperate for cash was a potential threat and liability. The owner became a Kingsley target, never a good thing to be.

The first forty-eight hours went off without a hitch. But then it started to get noisy, to borrow a military phrase meaning when everything goes to hell in a handbasket. Whitney was whisked off to a short promotional appointment, and in the client's temporary absence I prepared my team to maintain security at the rented house. However, Whitney's tour director, Roy Barnes, in a show of questionable wisdom that was oft repeated in the future, canceled the deployment, telling me to stand down my team until Whitney's return. Roy was a longtime friend of John Houston, Whitney's father and the president and CEO of Nippy Inc. Roy was short, round, diabetic, and a chronic smoker, who spoke and acted with John's authority. I tried to tell him that leaving the London house containing the client's personal effects unsecured was contrary to every security discipline imaginable, especially given our grave suspicions and reservations about the owner. Larry understood and concurred, but Roy was having none of it, and we were stood down.

A few days later I took an enraged call from Roy, complaining that there had been a massive security breach at the house. Sure enough, against all contractual stipulations, the owner had entered the house when it was not protected and had installed surveillance cameras, with the hope of filming Whitney and Robyn Crawford in a compromising lesbian interaction. This was based on rumors circulating about my principal and her longtime friend (by this point also her personal executive assistant). He was reportedly offering the most salacious images captured to the media for £1 million.

Fortunately, one of the newspapers in question had chosen to warn Whitney's people, but still, a story was about to hit the media and Roy was trying to pin the blame on me. His mistake was underestimating the Welsh in me. In no uncertain terms, which generally results in table-thumping to reinforce my point, I told him it was his decision not to protect the principal's property during her absence. It was his decision not to listen to the best in-country professional advice, and I left him in no doubt that I held him personally responsible for compromising the security of my principal. Both Larry and Tony

Bulluck, the tour manager, backed me to the hilt, agreeing that the house should never have been left without protection.

Unwittingly, and by their default, I was gaining a new level of respect in the eyes of the Nippy Inc. executives. The story did hit the press—minus photos or any proof, of course, but heavy with innuendo. John Houston flew to London to take the lead on a tour that was certainly not going as planned. Strictly speaking, this had not happened on my watch, but we had still come close to an incident that might well have ruined this gifted woman's career and destroyed my corporate reputation.

John was furious, though thankfully not with me. Quite the contrary. John was a gentleman, a worldly-wise individual, as comfortable with politicians as he was with hustlers (and he knew many of both). He had been around the block often. He also held a great love for and dedication to his daughter. It was John who'd given Whitney the nickname Nippy, for which the company that employed me was named. Apparently he had remarked of his toddler daughter that she was a "nippy one," as she was cute and fast on her feet. The name stuck, and everyone in her family and entourage called her Nippy or Nip. Out of professional deference I initially only addressed her as Ms. Houston. Whitney's father and I immediately forged a close rapport, and over time that grew into something rather special between us.

With the disastrous house rental situation behind us, and Whitney and her executive party safely installed in a more suitable hotel environment, we headed for her first UK show, at Wembley Stadium. It would be a tremendous challenge security-wise, for it was to be performed in a style known as "in the round," which effectively means a stage positioned in the very center of the giant arena, totally surrounded by concert attendees. Getting her to the stage was a melee beyond compare, the equivalent of a boxer making their way to the ring. It was chaotic and dangerous. It was also undignified, especially for a star of her stature, in my not-so-humble opinion.

My scope of duty was her UK security, but that didn't extend to the shows themselves. The show security team wasn't my call at the time, and frankly, they came off as sloppy and unprofessional. The men had no uniforms, or even uniformity, which created the impression that they were a bunch of knuckle-dragging amateurs. What they needed were smart black security-branded outfits so they could look the part, distinguish themselves when they needed to, and then fade into the shadows, remaining unseen but vigilant and ready to respond when appropriate. In fairness, the tour staff responsible for getting her to and from the stage had other functions on the tour, so their focus was easily diverted. They were not even security professionals, just big, muscular guys. I could see right away that this protocol needed to be upgraded to become safe, secure, planned, and professionally inviolable.

The show opened and I was in the wings. Listening to Whitney live for the first time, I was stunned. She was so much better onstage than on her CDs. Slim and beautiful, she had a melodious voice, with a range and volume that beggared belief coming from one so otherwise tiny. At points, she'd close her eyes and seem transported by a force that came through her in the form of a timbre so perfect, so strong and soulful, that it could warm even the coldest heart. And then she'd slowly open her eyes, come back to the audience, and beam out that smile that one couldn't help but return. Absolutely incredible.

2

One Moment in Time

As we left Wembley Stadium that night, I noticed we were being followed by a white Mercedes sports car with tinted windows. At that time Larry, the tour's security director, drove with the principal in the Rolls-Royce and I drove behind them, number two in the convoy, in a sleek V8 Porsche, one of the fruits of Churchill Security's success. Whitney's brother, Michael Houston, joined me as a passenger on this occasion. He was some kind of "road manager." As far as I could see, his role involved having as much fun as he could with as many people as he could.

Larry and I maintained radio communications throughout our journeys. I provided cover from any hostile approach from the rear, simultaneously being ever ready to power past and overtake the Rolls to place myself between any forward developing threats. It was a delicate balancing act, requiring one hundred percent concentration and vigilance. I also had to be ready to transfer the principal into my vehicle if hers became immobile for any reason, leaving all others behind to fend for themselves, if need be, including Whitney's beloved brother Michael.

After a couple of test maneuvers, I was left in no doubt that the Mercedes was pursuing us. I radioed Larry, advising of the threat and what action I intended to take. I told him not to stop but to continue driving to the Intercontinental Hotel, where I would join him after dealing with this developing nonsense. I waited until we reached the approach to a roundabout on the North Circular Road leading from Wembley Stadium. I slammed on the Porsche's brakes, trapping the Mercedes immediately behind me, as the principal's vehicle continued without pause. I could see Larry looking rearward. I leaped out of my car, sprinted back to where the Mercedes had been blocked by my vehicle, and tore open the driver's door. While the chap at the wheel was still in complete shock and before he could react, I'd incapacitated him and ripped the keys out of the ignition. I threw them across the dual carriageway into an area of exceptionally long grass. The two young men in the vehicle were in dumbfounded awe at the speed of what had just transpired. As I turned to leave, the driver wailed, with tears in his eyes, "It's my mum's car!" The wealthy, spoiled Greek boys explained they only wanted to "follow and party with Whitney."

I left them stranded in the middle of the road, blocking traffic coming behind them, went back to the Porsche, and headed for the hotel. The entire confrontation lasted less than two minutes. Michael Houston had never seen anything like it, and he was thrilled.

The word *fan* is a derivative of the Latin word *fanaticus*, meaning "insanely but divinely inspired." From it we get the word *fanatic*. As I was coming to realize, there was a thin dividing line between harmless fans, which those two guys tailing us claimed to be, and fans who might be dangerous, with intentions of carrying out some crazed obsession. If you let any fan, however seemingly innocent, get through your guard, they could turn out to be a killer. The golden rules were: never lose sight of your principal, and never let anyone get close enough to touch her.

After one of the Wembley shows, Whitney decided she wanted to relax and unwind by going to Browns nightclub in Holborn. This was not something she did very often. After a show, she generally was exhausted, hoarse, and ready for bed. I was horrified by the choice of venue and advised against it. Browns, a favorite spot for celebrities and the rich, had a reputation for drugs and trouble. Whitney could be compromised by negative publicity or allegations of drug use, and it was a certainty that the place would be infested with paparazzi.

As it happened, a good time was had by all inside the club. When the party emerged in the early hours I was positioned by Whitney's car. Word had spread that she was there, of course, and as predicted she was besieged by paparazzi. As Larry was slipping Whitney into the Rolls, a photographer attempted to open the rear passenger side door and clamber in alongside her. I approached him rapidly and we connected hard. He flew backward, slammed into the road, and slithered along on his back with pieces of his camera flying all over the road. The rest of the photographers present were absolutely thrilled, clicking their cameras to memorialize the scene of the fall of one of their own, with no apparent solidarity among colleagues. The following morning the pictures were all over the newspapers, showing me in a stance that would have made Bruce Lee proud, and the photographer hitting the road, his camera shattering.

We all had a good laugh at that one, but deep down I was disappointed that my advice against attending Browns nightclub had been ignored in the first place. Had it been heeded, the confrontation and consequent press could have been avoided. We were succeeding by default, not by my design, and that did not sit well with me. I was starting to earn the reputation of being a "physical" protection officer, which I generally was not. Diplomats and heads of commerce seldom attract any such level of threat.

As a Welshman, I do tend to let my emotions show. When I am angry, people definitely know it. Same goes when I'm sad or upset.

The attempted assaults on Whitney made me cross, and I am generally not a nice person when cross. But with Whitney and her entourage my reputation for ferocity seemed to go down surprisingly well.

It was at this time that Larry and I changed roles so that he could enjoy some time with his wife, who came to visit from Texas. I became the principal's CP officer on her hotel floor, and he moved to another location in the hotel with his wife. Now my room was directly opposite Whitney's. This arrangement was particularly appreciated by Ellen White, affectionately known as Aunt Bae, a childhood friend of Whitney's mother, Cissy Houston. Well into her sixties by then, Aunt Bae was Whitney's wardrobe director and surrogate mum. She was the wise elder of the group, the one to whom all deferred. Aunt Bae was a genuine and lovely person with a sterling soul. She and I ultimately developed an extremely strong mutual bond and rapport, as we both had the well-being of Whitney as our foremost objective. She was appreciative of my instinctive protection of and care for "her" Whitney. She was maternal, gregarious, and bags of fun.

In my view, Aunt Bae's love for Whitney surpassed that of her actual mother. Mrs. Cissy Houston, the vice president of Nippy Inc., was a force to be reckoned with, effectively more feared than revered. Though she was an astounding gospel singer with a tremendous voice in her own right, it became clear that, while proud, she was also envious of her daughter, and not always in a nice way. In her early twenties, Whitney had reached a level of fame that Cissy had spent a lifetime pursuing and failed to achieve, her claim to fame being a group background singer for Elvis Presley. Her angst was exacerbated by the story that because she was always on the road touring with Elvis, her husband John had been left to bring up the three children on his own. Despite her prolonged absences over the course of their childhoods, her children loved her deeply, especially Michael. But Whitney was showing signs of resentment for the power and control her mother sought to exercise over her.

There was none of that with Aunt Bae. She was a caregiver with no ulterior motive. Bae and I would watch Whitney sing together and she'd cry tears of happiness, saying, "Look, David, she'll turn right around now and lift her left leg." And Whitney would do precisely that at the exact time predicted by Bae. Aunt Bae knew her every move, on- and offstage.

As we became closer, Aunt Bae confided in me. She had suffered terrible tragedy in her life. She'd had three daughters, all of whom had fallen on hard times. One had gone missing and was presumed dead. Bae made it clear to me that she was happy to have me around to help safeguard Whitney from the ills that had assailed her daughters. "David, you are exactly what Whitney needs right now, someone as professional as you."

———————

As Larry moved on to planning advance security for the rest of the European tour, I became Whitney's lead CP and de facto "bullet catcher." After the room change, I was on call 24/7 to all the ladies of the executive party who occupied the floor. My door was always open. Literally. Very quickly, Whitney realized she could step outside her room at any time of the day or night and I would be there. Always. Going anywhere in or out of the hotel, I'd stick rigidly to her, never leaving her side, slightly distancing myself so as not to overcrowd her by my proximity. She apparently found that unusual and refreshing, but to me it was the very essence of close protection and allowed me the best opportunity to do the job I was trained and hired to do.

Closer to the heart of things now, I realized that Whitney's tour group gained everything from her. They had little power or repute as individuals unless they claimed to the crowd or person they wanted to impress that they were Whitney's bassist, drummer, guitarist, or dancer—and they would do so regardless of their real role in the tour. Everything flowed from her. That acclaimed association earned them booze, drugs, other freebies, and women, which may otherwise not have been available to them. All they had to do was use the magic word: *Whitney.*

One member of Whitney's entourage who stood out was her personal assistant, Silvia Vejar. Originally from El Salvador, Silvia was in her twenties and had a young daughter who often stayed with her mother in New Jersey. Short in stature and sweet and quiet in nature, Silvia looked after all of Whitney's personal matters 24/7. She worked like a dog and was loyalty personified. It became clear that Silvia was close to Whitney, and especially to her brother Michael. Silvia was ever present, but not one to party or seek out recognition from Whitney.

I had no need for that either. Quite the contrary: a CP operative doesn't like being in the limelight. I sought the shadows and eschewed attention in all its forms. Whitney noticed and appreciated me. She began to rely on me. "What does David say?" she'd ask. "If David says it's OK, let's do it."

And I had certainly noticed her. Whitney turned the stereotypes I had developed after long years policing London's streets upside down. I'd expected her to be all about sex, drugs, and rock 'n' roll—party, party, party. She was not. Her entourage partied, but generally she stayed in or around her room, which often left the two of us in close proximity. She and I could talk on almost any subject. In the Rolls-Royce together, in the hotel restaurant, visiting her favorite Chinese restaurant in Grosvenor Square, in the doorway of my room or hers . . . we talked. She possessed a ladylike grace coupled with an amazing sense of fun. There was a conflicting old-school shyness and lack of impropriety about her. In short, I was captivated by this gorgeous young lady.

In those days I was super fit, accustomed to running at least five miles as a simple daily workout routine. I'd kill time working out in my hotel room, using the furniture as exercise aids. I'd rehearse aikido katas on the thick carpets of the hotel corridors. It got noticed.

The rumor was that I had previously looked after the British Royal Family. That was not quite the truth, but I kept my mouth shut. With my dry Welsh wit and self-effacing British sense of humor, I made Whitney laugh. Some CP guys have a tendency to promote themselves beyond their worth. I do the opposite. I would mock myself mercilessly, accentuating how my naive and archaic Britishness kept getting me into trouble. Whitney loved it.

As my relationship with her developed, she became relaxed and playful with me. We'd walk into a public venue like an airport lounge—always the zone of greatest threat, because it was there that I could do the least preparatory assessment and had minimal environmental control—and I'd tap her on the shoulder. "Boss, take the bloody headphones off. If something happens you won't be able to hear me telling you to run." She'd do as asked, but I'd know she was cross. She'd leave one of the earpads on and squint at me sideways, just to make her point.

In the CP world becoming close with the principal is acceptable, especially with regard to nonverbal communication in scenarios where there is no opportunity to talk. In a sense, you have to admire and revere your principal to be willing to die for him or her. But that was as far as it could be allowed to go. If you ever crossed the line into intimate relations with your protectee, the CP-principal connection was compromised. If he looks at the principal and sees a woman he loves and knows sexually, the protector becomes a liability, losing perspective. And, more important, he becomes the victim of a reduced level of environmental and situational awareness. The smitten CP operative is rendered impotent and useless.

I have seen it happen with other security professionals and their charges. In one particular case that springs to mind, a security officer became involved with his famous protectee and eventually fathered her child—but at least in that case the operative was professional enough to immediately stop acting as personal security, becoming something else entirely, for as long as that lasted. I knew all of this, but still had a mind and an imagination.

———————

The tour group left London and headed north to Birmingham. In the hotel foyer after the first show, the entourage began a spontaneous jam session, led by John Simmons, a Black man with a slight build who served as Whitney's superlative director of music at the time. Simmons took a seat at the hotel's grand piano and began to play. Singers and assorted musicians soon joined in. For the guests this was a bonus like no other, but the hotel manager didn't quite see it that way. He marched over and told Simmons to stop playing. It was then that Whitney's father stepped in. John Houston confronted the manager and announced that he'd buy the piano—hell, he'd buy the entire hotel if he had to—but Simmons was going to play. Simmons played and we all had a great time. I suspect some of the snobbish guests at that top-notch hotel had complained. While John understood the hotel staff's response to be an expression of racism and took his stand, I thought it could simply be because our group was loud, drunk, and rowdy.

Another such encounter took place when we flew back to London, where Whitney was scheduled to record "One Moment in Time" for the forthcoming Olympics in Seoul. I had developed a streamlined system of travel whereby I would take charge of the executive party's passports and personally interact with the authorities on departure and landing. I was dealing with a customs officer who sought clarification over a stamp in one of the passports. On seeing this interaction between myself and the customs officer, Michael Houston, interpreting it as contentious, burst forth with a tirade, accusing the White officer of discriminating against them because they were Black. I was astounded and embarrassed, considering the officer's question innocuous and of no real significance. In resolving the issue and restoring the equilibrium, I realized then that race would always play a role in working with Whitney and her group.

I had never been exposed to the perspective of African Americans. I learned that no matter who I was, to many—especially in the younger generation—I was White and therefore not to be trusted, often to be disliked outright, whether I had personally earned that distinction or not. I understood this to be a result of the daily trials and tribulation of life in the United States. I worked hard to be accepted, and I think I earned the respect of those with whom I became close.

One day we drove to a studio on Oxford Street for the recording of Whitney's song "One Moment in Time." I remained in the green-room preparing a cup of coffee and a snack. Before I had finished it, Whitney was out of the studio and we were on our way back to the hotel, by way of a McDonald's drive-through (one of Whitney's favorite edible pleasures). As the singular McDonald's smell of fried potatoes and grease wafted through the Rolls, I wondered what had happened, anticipating that something had gone terribly wrong in the studio to prevent the recording. When we got back to the hotel, I asked Whitney's friend Robyn if everything was OK. She replied, "David, there's a reason she's called One-Take Houston. She goes in, records, and walks out." That song, which took advantage of Whitney's incredible soulful strength and four-octave range, became a number-one hit and an integral part of her musical legacy. It took less than fifteen minutes to record.

———

The last show Whitney performed in London during that tour was the Nelson Mandela 70th Birthday Tribute concert on June 11, 1988. Wembley Stadium was the selected venue, an outdoor event on what turned out to be a chilly day, even for June in England. It was an unfor-gettable show. Whitney, bundled in a turtleneck, sequined jacket, and black leather gloves, the wind whipping through her hair, captured all hearts with eight songs, including three encores. Also performing for the occasion were Dire Straits, Stevie Wonder, Sting, Tracy Chapman, the Eurythmics, UB40, and Meat Loaf, to whom I was introduced and spontaneously addressed as "Mr. Loaf," much to the amusement of all present.

Stevie Wonder had a serious problem in that someone had forgotten to pack his Synclavier, which reportedly carried his entire twenty-five-minute intended show of synthesized music, and without which he would have had to announce he could not perform. He was led backstage, literally in tears. Whitney, however, ultimately saved the day by allowing him to use her equipment and sound engineers, and by helping him to shout to his band for each chord change, for which they would usually rely on the missing Synclavier.

Whitney and Stevie were close friends, and our paths would cross with his over the years at various concert venues the world over. I was somewhat bemused by the tale that whenever his group booked a hotel, his manager took the best suites and Stevie had the smaller ones, the idea being that Stevie would never know the difference because he was visually challenged. Heaven alone knows whether there is any truth to such rumor. Just one of those industry idiosyncrasies. Every artist has a tale to tell about another. Suffice it to say, he was an absolute sweetheart, and even if that rumor was true, I do not for one moment believe he would have been fazed by it.

All things eventually come to an end, and the UK leg of the 1988 European tour was no exception. My team and I started planning our return to other security commitments. On the second-to-last day in London, Larry took me aside and told me that he wanted me personally to perform all the advance security work for and throughout the remaining European tour.

By that time, my initial misgivings had vanished. Yes, with this group one had to throw the textbook out the window and learn to

fly by the seat of one's pants, being ever ready for the numerous confrontations that would surely arise. Yes, Whitney and her entourage
were a CP's nightmare, being diametrically opposed and totally at odds
with any semblance of security awareness and discipline. Individually,
however, they were some of the nicest and sweetest people I had ever
met in my life. I accepted Larry's offer, and thus started a European
and Scandinavian tour.

———————

I first experienced Whitney's indefatigable joy of spirit in Copenhagen,
where we visited the vast and world-renowned Tivoli Gardens amusement park. Loving nothing more than to laugh and have fun, Whitney
enjoyed the roller coaster above all else. Personally, roller-coaster rides
have always been a no-go for me. My hope that Larry would participate, having reverted to lead CP for the European leg of the tour,
was dashed immediately, because that ride in particular was a no-go
for him as well. Someone had to accompany the principal into this
insecure environment, and I had no choice but to defer to the pref-
erences of Larry, both my superior and my elder.

It was "crap or get off the pot" time, and to the amusement of
all, in that I had voiced very loudly and in no uncertain terms my
total trepidation of such contraptions, it was Whitney and me in the
front carriage, with the rest of the crew spread out behind us. I found
myself cursing and muttering under my breath on the slow journey
up into the clouds, and screaming profanities all the way down to
where it seemed the only respite would be the opening of the gates
to hell itself, into which I would gratefully be swallowed. Whitney
was cracking up, with tears streaming down her face, and no one was
happier than I was when the damned thing came to an end. But my
relief was short-lived, as Whitney wanted to go again. And again. And
we did. I think I aged about a decade during the fifteen minutes or

so we were engaged in what for Whitney was an absolute pleasure, probably enhanced by my total anguished and profane displeasure. By the third time around I had conquered my fear but didn't let on. I was very much playing to the captive audience. And loving it.

I got the feeling that Robyn relished the fact that I initially did not enjoy the event. Although I did not mind being the target of their fun, with Robyn it seemed to be something more. She reveled in the discomfort of those to whom Whitney showed favor. Robyn eventually came out as a proud gay woman, but at that time she was very much in the closet. She loved Whitney with a passion, but as far as I could tell, the feeling was not reciprocated by Whitney to the same extent. As Whitney and I grew closer, I found myself increasingly shunned by Robyn.

After the roller coaster, Robyn and some other band members leaped upon a cylindrical machine that rotated faster and faster, forcing the occupants bodily against the internal wall by centrifugal pressure, and then up it so their feet were no longer in contact with any surface. It then went from spinning the riders horizontally to spinning them even faster vertically. There was no one more pleased than I to see Robyn wobbling off that contraption at the end, green in the face and sick as a dog.

I parted company with Whitney and the tour group in Switzerland. I had developed a close bond with Michael, Aunt Bae, John, and even tour director Roy. Larry and I had forged a friendship that would last a lifetime.

"David, don't go too far. You'll be hearing from us," Aunt Bae said on bidding farewell. A similar sentiment was expressed by Robyn, of all people. Even so, I assumed that by the time this lot moved on to their next touring adventure, I would be merely a fading memory.

I had thoroughly enjoyed the perpetual motion of advance threat assessment through Europe, but enough was enough. It had been an interesting journey, yet not one I would be looking to repeat anytime soon, my diplomatic and commercial clients being just fine, and not nearly as complicated as moving an extremely fluid and undisciplined group around the world. I was proud to have represented the combined ever-evolving training of the Metropolitan Police with the Special Air Service in the specific discipline of close personal protection. I'd been hired to do a job, and I'd kept Whitney safe in the UK and assured continuity through Europe. Life was about to return to normal. I suspect I was trying to convince myself there wasn't something that I was already starting to miss.

3

I Will Love You Always

In July 1988, I was driving north on the M1 motorway to attend meetings in Wales when my car phone rang. "Hey, Dave! Dave, this is Roy Barnes. Dave, we want you to take charge of our security for Whitney's Far East tour."

I was shocked, bowled over in fact. We then lost signal and the call was cut before I could even begin to think of a response. These were the early days of cell phone technology with yards of wires installed in the Porsche to make a briefcase-sized cell phone work. For a moment, as the gentle green hills of my homeland whizzed by, I thought he was not going to call back. But he did. Roy asked me to name my price. I thought of a ridiculous number and doubled it. He didn't hesitate in telling me they were happy to pay. By the end of the call, I had committed to three months touring Japan, Australia, Taiwan, Hong Kong, and Hawaii.

This assignment was to be very different from the service I had provided previously. Larry Wansley had returned to his post as director of security for the Dallas Cowboys and would not be with us. Furthermore, I would not have my British team with me. Therefore, I immediately set out to begin preplanning, international risk evaluation,

and threat assessments in what were, to me, alien operational environments. I flew in advance to Japan, where the tour was scheduled to
begin, and used the time to run practice scenarios with the Japanese
staff and to pre-advance venues. I had never worked in Asia before
and was eager to learn about the culture and challenges that might
need to be handled.

I met our driver Yoshi and my interpreter Koko, and we went
through vehicle embarking and disembarking drills. We practiced parking, remaining in the vehicle with the engine running, and resisting
the urge to follow their natural and instinctive protocol, which would
be to get out of the vehicle and open all doors for everyone before
getting back in. Japanese working in the service industry are truly the
politest people I have ever encountered, so it was entirely alien for them
to remain in a vehicle and not be the last to get in. Yoshi eventually
got the hang of it, and he became a more aggressive driver at my
urging. Yoshi, Koko, and I ended up having a lot of fun. Over the
years I spent more than four months in Japan touring with Whitney
and came to love the country and its people.

The culture in Japan is significantly more disciplined than that in
Western countries but posed its own level of fanaticism, with frenet-
ically and physically emotional fans whose strength came mainly in
volume. Every gathering of fans was a potential riot waiting to happen. The roadways in Japan added a new definition to congestion, at
best proving to be the world's largest barely moving car park. Timed
travel calculations became important in the planning of all external
maneuvers between hotels, venues, and airports. Add to that the rainy
season, and the annual sumo wrestlers competition in Tokyo, and the
journey to and from a venue could take longer than the show itself.

As the tour progressed through Japan, we arrived at our hotel in
Kyoto. We got off the elevator on our floor to find that the door to
the first room we passed was open. Sitting on the bed was a young
man holding a rose. Trouble! I placed the executive party in their

rooms and contacted hotel management to remove him from our floor. It had been a stipulation on booking the hotel that no rooms on our floor would be given to anyone outside our party. My request was ever so politely and positively received, with all due apologies and an absolute assurance that the young man had been spoken with and would not approach our party and, more specifically, Ms. Houston. However, when we left that evening for the show, there he was again, sitting on his bed, holding the rose, saying nothing. I stopped in the doorway to the room, leaving him no option should he have been thinking of leaving the room, until our party had safely passed.

That night, after another incredibly successful show, Whitney, Silvia, Robyn, and I returned to the hotel. As we walked across the expansive foyer there was a scream, and I would swear to this day it was the word *Banzai!*—a traditional Japanese battle cry. I turned toward the noise and there he was, my chap from the bedroom with the rose. He was on the run, hurtling in our direction from the far end of the foyer, screaming and holding a bunch of flowers outstretched in one hand.

I immediately told Robyn to get Whitney into the elevator and went, at equal speed, to meet our lunatic attacker. As I saw the ladies hustling into the elevator, the man and I clashed at some speed and force. Encouraged by my rugby-tackle shoulder, he bounced rearward, his bunch of flowers landing beyond in a mess of stalks and petals. I was on him in seconds and stopped him physically, but not his screams.

The hotel management was mortified. This lad had embarrassed them beyond words. They dragged him to his feet, shouted at him, and then slapped him, at which point I started to feel sorry for the kid. While all this was going on, I examined the flowers, finding the disarrayed content clean of sharp objects, noxious substances, recording devices, or offensive matter—always a possibility when people sought to hand flowers to Whitney. Leaving the staff and the young chap to work it out, which they did loudly, with much pushing and shoving and total subservience on the part of the offender, I went up to our floor and explained what had happened. We all had a good laugh about it but also understood it to be another lesson learned.

While we were talking together on the landing, an assortment of staff came straight into the young chap's room, and within moments my earlier request to have him moved came to pass with no further ceremony. Thinking that was the end of the matter, I was surprised when I received a call from the manager asking me to please meet him in the foyer. Arriving there, I saw the young man, now totally dejected, surrounded by hotel officials and an older couple who turned out to be his parents. A few minutes of the most profuse (and embarrassing to me) apologies followed, proffered by the boy's father and translated by the hotel staff, with both father and mother bowing continuously. The son was apparently "in love" with Whitney, meant her no harm, and merely wished to show the depth of his love by presenting her with flowers. The parents accepted full responsibility and blame for the "shame" their son had brought upon their family. The youth just stood there, head hung low, and did not participate in the conversation.

Whitney loved and appreciated her fans. She always made sure to thank them at every concert and whenever speaking in public. However, when fans became obsessed, you could never tell if they were dangerous or harmless. As her CP officer, I would not be doing my job if I didn't always err on the side of dangerous.

Whitney would always take a singing break mid-show, during which she'd introduce her musicians, singers, and dancers while the band members continued to play, each taking a solo. At the Yokohama Arena during her breather, Whitney called me onstage and introduced me as her bodyguard. At first I didn't move, being both mortified and paralyzed. But she persisted, and I stepped out of the wings to the roar of the crowd. I engaged in a dojo-type bow without ever losing visual contact with Whitney's smiling eyes, and retreated, at which time I realized I had not taken a breath for some thirty seconds.

Only then did I exclaim "Fuck!" to the shock of all present. Now some thirty thousand fans knew precisely who I was. Any hope of remaining clandestine when seen in the company of Whitney was destroyed. But by the same token, something changed. She had recognized me as important to her. That realization sparked my pride and reinforced the knowledge that there was nothing I would not do to protect this young woman.

From there she moved on to the gospel portion of her show, and my sentiments toward her only strengthened. When she sang the hymns she was raised on, Whitney was transformed. As the backup singers' voices swelled into a crescendo, she'd close her eyes, raise her hand to the sky, and draw out note after perfect note, bottom lip quaking with her effort. A certain vein in her neck often looked as if it were going to burst as she belted out the words. You could feel it right down to your bone marrow. I'm not a religious man, but even I could see that her song was her prayer, a vehicle for both her pain and her strength, and her voice carried it to the hearts of all who heard her.

In the car on the way back to the hotel after the show, she joked about having called me out onstage. Glancing in the passenger-side rearview mirror that our cars were outfitted with, I could see the anger on Robyn's face. She had never been called onstage or introduced. In that instant, the dynamic of my relationship with Robyn went sour. She was jealous of how Whitney felt about me, and that jealousy could only have been because she saw what she interpreted as Whitney's feelings or perhaps love for another. That night I was placed in Robyn's crosshairs.

———————

Normally, after a show, Whitney would stay in her room and speak on the phone for hours with her then-boyfriend, Eddie Murphy. On the evenings when she didn't perform, she loved to go to the Tony Roma's restaurant near our hotel in Tokyo. One night, after such a meal, we returned to find Michael Houston in the hotel foyer together with Gary Garland, Whitney's half-brother, who was to be a new addition to the tour.

The son of Cissy Houston and a former partner of hers, Gary had been brought up by John Houston as if he were his own son. Six-foot-four and at one time a budding basketball star, Gary could have been in the same league as Magic Johnson and the like, but he'd compromised himself and squandered that opportunity. He made it to the NBA, playing for the Denver Nuggets, but after one season he'd reportedly tested positive for drugs and was taken off the team. Since then, he'd become one of those I-could-have-been-a-contender types.

He had proceeded through his life thereafter with what I perceived to be the attitude of a victim. Gary was a very competent singer by any standard—to my mind, a crooner. His version of Luther Vandross's "A House Is Not a Home" was superlative, and his solos were always impressive, as was his participation as a background singer. Gary was also a bit of a problem child. Special permissions had been sought and acquired to secure the essential visas to facilitate his ability to travel to and perform in Japan with his sister. Because he had prior felony drug convictions, a condition of the granting of that visa was regular urine tests while in the country. If he failed a test, he would be immediately thrown out of Japan. Through the tour grapevine I heard a story that to pass the tests, one of the traveling entourage members, who was not a drug user, supplied Gary with a sample of urine that he strapped to the top of his leg. True or not, Gary's ability to manipulate situations to his own advantage became legendary.

In the hotel foyer, Gary and Michael were engaged in conversation with a Japanese couple, a young woman and her grandmother, who looked every bit over a century in age. Whitney broke ranks and ran to greet and hug her brothers. While she was being introduced to the younger woman, and as I approached, the old crone started speaking, and then, to the shock and amazement of all present, she went into a half spin, extended an arm, and smashed Whitney in her back. Whitney was propelled into her brothers, and the grandma started shouting hysterically with her granddaughter attempting to placate her. My interpreter Koko was not with me at that moment. Unable to understand what the two were saying, the display was completely incomprehensible and random to us.

Avoiding the instinct to respond and severely remonstrate with any such attacker, I hustled Whitney to the elevator. She was unhurt, thankfully, and we laughed during the journey up and back to her room.

Taking the bullet train to travel through Japan was a memorable experience that provided an opportunity for downtime when the band members and dancers all interacted directly with Whitney and the executive party. It was a time for memory making, photographs, conversation, and jam sessions; fun on-the-move occasions. Our group was large enough to effectively take up a carriage by ourselves, or otherwise completely surround Whitney, thereby protecting her from any indirect approach. Intrusion by non–tour members in the form of other passengers was a rare issue as our Japanese tour staff manned each side of the carriage to deter would-be autograph hunters. With this extra buffer of protection, I was able to relax and enjoy myself a bit more than usual.

I was told that Whitney liked to provide opportunities to up-and-coming young people in the music industry, and thus many of the band members and dancers were unknowns, kids from the neighborhood debuting their talents with her show. They were generally nice kids, focused and dedicated to their music, and their performances onstage were generally superlative. Many did not return for subsequent tours, however, and nothing was ever said. If you were not there at that time, you did not exist, nor had you ever. That was the way it was on the road.

For the Japanese, waiting for the bullet train is a strictly disciplined affair. There are boxes and lines painted on the floor to stand in and wait, designed to avoid any potential for blocking the train doors at the appropriate times. The Japanese commuters packed those boxes like sardines, creating the impression that they were never to step over the painted lines for fear of certain and terrible torture and death.

On one occasion we were waiting in a somewhat more loosely packed fashion when I felt Whitney lean against me, link her arm through mine, and place her head on my left shoulder. I could sense her presence and even the beating of her heart. She was that close. I stood there conflicted, unable and unwilling to move out of such an intimate interaction. Self-consciously, I suspected that others in our group noticed something different, not exactly a bodyguard with his principal, and out came the cameras. Robyn joined us and leaned on my right shoulder. This head-on-shoulder moment was a friendship indicator well beyond the scope and parameters of a professional rapport, and for that moment in time I enjoyed it immensely.

Another such moment came toward the end of the Japan leg of the tour when our hosts threw a party for us. Duly attired in suit and tie, I proudly escorted Whitney to the event. She was dressed in a body-hugging silver minidress and looked stunning. Later into the evening Whitney sashayed over to me. She took my hand.

"Let's dance, David," she murmured.

Who was I to demur? "Yes, boss."

It was a slow song and demanded that's how we should dance. I held her close, as dictated by the melody, then closer. As the crowd snapped photos, I reminded myself that I worked best behind the scenes. I didn't like to be in the limelight, and this type of visual imagery made me feel uncomfortable. For this one night, though, I enjoyed the special closeness with my principal.

I needed Whitney to be able to depend totally on my ability to protect her and to respond to my directions, no questions asked. She needed someone with absolute professional detachment, and with her well-being fully at heart. I knew by now that I was that man. We danced together and she had lots of fun, as she did when she was exclusively in the company of those she considered friends rather than record executives, groupies, press, or others whose connection to her was self-serving in one way or another. That night and that dance consolidated our relationship, rooting it in a deep level of trust.

By the end of the Japan segment of the tour, Whitney and I had developed a unique rapport, one that often required no speaking at all—which is exactly what is needed for maximum close-protection effectiveness. One cannot risk timely delays by talking. Look, signal, act, and react, as one. At promotional events she would look right at me a certain way through the crowd, and that was my signal. *Come and get me out of here.* Off I would go to the stage, take her hand and walk her off, often to the surprise of others. In a crowd, moving to a hotel or show, or at an airport, I in the lead, she would tug and hold onto the rear of my jacket, signaling me not to stop, to get her out of there.

Even onstage while performing, she would see something in the crowd that she knew I could not see, as I always stood to her left, in the shadows, slammed by the volume output of numerous coffin-sized speakers that years later ultimately contributed vastly to the ruination of my hearing, and she would simply look over at me and then at what she had noticed, so I knew to react. Often onstage, I would see her cast a glance in my direction, as if making sure I was there and watching. I always was.

The special nonverbal communication between Whitney and me caused angst for many who could not communicate with her in the same way or at the same level. Effectively, nobody had quite the same connection with Whitney as I had when we worked together. Not only was she kept safe, but more important, she *knew* she was safe. And I knew I was doing my job well.

———————

After the final show in Yokohama Arena, we drove back to the hotel. On this drive, as with every road move, I rode in the front passenger seat, with the principal diagonally positioned in the rear seat directly behind Yoshi, our driver. From that position, I could easily launch myself over the seat and land on top of her to protect her against anything incoming. With my own rearview mirror I was well sighted, more so in many instances than the actual driver. With that placement we could talk and I could make eye contact via the mirror, without having to turn around and away from any threat approaching from our direction of travel.

Theoretically, if someone shot at the car, my role was to position to avoid the principal being struck, even if it meant being incapacitated myself. I had been through hours of dedicated and repetitive training so that rather than duck and hide, the natural instinct, my instinct was melded and manipulated and eventually became to launch myself over into the back, to shield the principal. If I hadn't been prepared mentally and physically to do that, I'd have been in a different line of work. With such threats, the objective was to put distance between the attacker and the principal. Absent the ability to do so, I would have to take the fight to the assailant at speed. By contrast, my chauffeurs always knew their job was to drive and only to drive. No driver of mine would leave his seat or switch off the vehicle's engine until the principal and I were out and safe. No driver would open any door of the vehicle upon arrival, but would sit there, engine running and in low gear with all doors locked, until I had confirmed the area was safe and given the signal to unlock the doors so I could extract the principal.

Returning to a vehicle, the car would be in place in advance, engine running, doors locked. On my approach, the driver would engage the gears, unlock the doors, and wait. The principal would be inserted in the rear behind the driver, and I would walk quickly around to the passenger side and thrust my backside into the seat, by which time I expected us to be moving. The last things I would place in the car would be my feet. Everyone knows the scenario where you try to enter a moving car by placing a foot on the floorboards and you end up hopping down the road like a fool. Throw your backside in the seat and your legs will always follow.

On that long drive back to Tokyo, Whitney must have heard me singing. I tend to subconsciously hum or whistle, and I'm the last person to realize I'm doing it, often to my embarrassment. She eyed me in the mirror.

"You know, David, you have perfect pitch."

Being at first totally oblivious to what she meant, and then mortified that she had heard me, I responded, "Thank you very much, boss. I tend to only do it in the bathroom. Sing, I mean." She laughed. As usual, Robyn rode alongside Whitney in the backseat. I noticed through the mirror and from the daggers that were being slammed into my back through the seat that tonight Robyn wasn't smiling much. Whitney said that she wanted to sign a tour program for me when we got back to the hotel, to say thank you that Japan had gone so well. A little later Robyn brought it to my room. She had a face like thunder. She dumped the program and left.

I knew Robyn was pissed. The seed of discontent had been sown when Whitney introduced me onstage as her bodyguard. Robyn was always testing the love between herself and Whitney. To me her behavior seemed insecure and overly protective, as if the rapport between

Whitney and me were a serious threat to her. As if she feared losing not just Whitney's love but also her status and sense of control. If so, that was all in her mind, but in such close quarters, it was not something that could be ignored or overlooked without the potential for serious repercussions.

Once Robyn had left, I opened the program. The words written on it left me speechless and even more conflicted:

> *David—What can I say? I will love you always.*
> *P.S. You've got a friend.*

This was several years before she would record the song "I Will Always Love You" for the movie *The Bodyguard*.

4

Uncle Weeder

On October 19, 1988, we traveled to Sydney, Australia. Upon arrival at our hotel, Robyn told me I was to stay in my room on Whitney's orders. *What?* Whitney's personal attorney, Sheldon Platt, had advised of a potentially dangerous fan living in Sydney. The threat needed to be confronted rapidly and effectively, something I could not do while confined to my room. How could this world-renowned star allow herself to be swayed by Robyn's jealousy in such a way as to put her own life in danger?

I sat in the hotel room frustrated and fuming. By the third day, the ridiculousness of the situation had to be confronted. I announced to the executives at Nippy Inc. in Fort Lee, New Jersey, via facsimile, that as I was being precluded from fulfilling my role, and the principal was being exposed to danger in consequence, I felt I had no alternative but to resign and leave.

At this point, I learned that no one else knew of Robyn's efforts to erode the principal's confidence in me. John Houston intervened, and Robyn was suitably chastised. I later found out that what I had experienced with Robyn was nothing new, according to the executives. She was considered a thorn in their sides, and they hated the hold she had over Whitney, taking the position that her passionate personal friendship was at odds with her professional competence. The family's animosity toward Robyn ran deep.

Gary Garland, Whitney's half-brother, was wholly ill-disposed to Robyn's existence on the planet, let alone her proximity to and effect upon Whitney. On one occasion I had to stand between them as they circled one another, Gary seeming fully intent on beating her to a pulp. Robyn, fearing the possibility that she had pushed his buttons one too many times, positioned herself in the hopes that I would protect her from a direct all-out assault. Whitney intervened by screaming at them from the tour bus, and the potentially explosive scene was diffused. At least until the next time.

In Australia everyone took my side, to Robyn's detriment, such was the extent of truly negative feelings so many held against her.

Once released from my hotel room, I was able to address the threat to which Sheldon had alerted us. Sheldon was an incredible negotiator and entertainment industry specialist, a wiry legal talent beyond compare, and without whom Whitney's career would have been more compromised than any will ever know or appreciate. He had advised of some disgusting mailings Whitney's fan club had received at the corporate office in Fort Lee, including underwear and socks grossly soiled with various bodily fluids, coupled with handwritten notes from one John Quinlan of Sydney. He was a deranged character waiting for Whitney to arrive and perform there. He quoted her song "Greatest Love of All" and expressed a determination to take Whitney "to meet his dead mother" where they would thereafter "live forever as a family."

To have denied Quinlan access to the show would have resulted in potential bad publicity for the principal. In the entertainment industry there is always a conflict between privacy and publicity. In this instance, a workable compromise was achieved. Quinlan remained under surveillance pending our return to Sydney from Perth, for a series of final shows there before leaving for Hong Kong. Working closely with the Sydney Police, arrangements were made for plain-clothes officers to be seated around the purchased seat assigned to Quinlan, to react in case he should make any attempt to carry out his threat to take Whitney to meet his dead mother. At the concert, and in somewhat of an anticlimax, he sat there, watched the show, and when Whitney sang "Greatest Love of All," his cue, he was motionless. At the end he stood up, walked out, and was never seen nor heard from again. The Sydney police officers were thanked for their assistance. They had enjoyed the free show, in any event.

In reality, there was good cause to be wary of this stalker, as during the show he was totally impassive: he did not clap, rise, jump up and down, or express any form of emotion whatsoever. So even if he had not announced his intent in advance, he would have been selected for special attention by me and the security team because of this rather unusual body language "tell."

—————————

We headed to Canberra for another show. As usual, the tour management staff and I sat down to prepare and advance the environment and venue. During this meeting Michael Houston announced the long-awaited arrival of Uncle Weeder, who was apparently due the next day. Understanding that Americans have some unusual names, I asked Michael whether I should prepare credentials for him to gain access to backstage and other exclusive environments. The group burst out laughing, and it was clear they were laughing at me. Confused, I asked why and was duly enlightened that "Uncle Weeder" was a euphemism for weed, marijuana, cannabis, or any other name by which one cares to call the herbal drug.

Interestingly, this was the first overt indication I had received of the potential use of drugs around my principal. As I joined in with their laughter at my naïveté, on the inside I was displeased by what I perceived as a myriad of unwarranted dangers: illegal drugs, the unknown individuals who would bring them into our secure environment, the exposure of the principal to unwanted publicity associated with their use, the inferences that could be drawn by the media, and so forth.

My concerns were vast and escalating, but it seemed these were issues that I personally had to mull over and deal with, as it was clear certain of the staff thought this was an acceptable and entirely normal part of their culture, issues of legality being little more than a minor hindrance. It filled me with dread. Was this the "drugs" element of the sex, drugs, and rock 'n' roll to which I had always been strongly opposed? I believe the group noticed my clear aversion to the concept, because if said "Uncle Weeder" showed up the following day, I was not, nor was I ever, formally introduced to him.

On Wednesday, October 26, we flew from Canberra to the turquoise sea and powder sands of Perth, on the western coast of Australia. There, the tour group members were invited to a party at our hotel. Whitney attended briefly but soon left to avoid the attention she was getting from the people not associated with our group. I was glad to leave them to their drinking and carousing.

Very early the next morning, my phone began to ring. It was Tony Bulluck, the tour manager, letting me know that a local woman had reported being gang-raped. She named a member of Whitney's entourage as the leader and the person directly responsible for her sexual assault. I recall having seen the woman at the party the previous evening. She was a tall woman in her thirties, with long blonde hair, clearly affected by whatever she was drinking or smoking, and she had attracted the attention of the men in our group, many of whom were there with their tongues hanging out.

Damage control mode!

My responsibility was to consider the impact such a dreadful allegation would have on Whitney. The possibilities were incalculable, and clearly never a thought for those of our party who would act questionably, irresponsibly, or downright illegally. I gathered as much information as I could from brief interviews with the tour staff who had attended the party, many of whom were still stupefied from the effects of the night before. But being accused of rape tended to sober most of them up. They responded to my questions while casting quick glances at pictures of their wives or girlfriends, with whose photographs they invariably traveled.

The consensus was that the woman had become drunk and had reportedly willingly gone away with the accused and no one else, returning later to continue partying with the others. Regardless of what had actually happened, it was not something that Whitney should have to deal with, considering the damage an alleged scandal could have caused her. The tabloids, so keen to build up a star like Whitney only so they could start tearing her down piece by piece, would have had a field day. Very few of the touring party ever thought in terms of their actions having the potential to destroy the reputation of the principal upon whom they relied for their fiscal well-being.

I reached out to Sheldon Platt in New York and explained the predicament. He was unperturbed, and I sensed he'd been here before. He contacted a local barrister named Rodney Anderson to run defense with the local police, who were expected to be at the hotel any minute. Sheldon and I had come to know each other during the time Whitney was first in the UK, and he had written to me specifically stating how much the executives had appreciated my professionalism and inestimable assistance during the UK and European tours.

Whitney was told of the developments after the fact, accepting the allegations and the action taken. It struck me that no one was surprised or fazed by what had happened.

Mr. Anderson managed to successfully defer and deflect intended police activity away from the principal. The barrister did the job he'd been hired to do, which was to protect the principal's reputation at all costs. Apart from anything else, her name was the brand from which so many made so much. The lawyers were there to protect the brand, and by entrenched association, the Houston family, even if one of the entourage had done something wrong.

During our Australian tour, as with many others, Whitney diverted her time and attention to some of the children's charities she sponsored around the world. Whitney was an amazingly gracious soul, in tune with the needs and sensibilities of others, especially her global family of children. So arrangements were made for her to visit a children's ward and spend some time with the seriously ill and debilitated youngsters.

As we approached the hospital entrance, beads of sweat began to form on my forehead. I tried to breathe deeply but could only manage shallow, insufficient attempts at taking in air. I stopped.

"Boss, I don't think I can go in."

"What do you mean, David?"

Haltingly, I shared some of my personal life with her. When my daughter, Sara, was three, I used to walk with her on the paths through London's Hampstead Heath, near where we lived in the neighborhood of Belsize Park. It used to frustrate me that after no more than a hundred yards at a time she would turn to me and plead, "Daddy, Daddy, pick me up. Please pick me up." There were occasions when I fear I reduced her to tears trying to make her walk for greater distances than her little legs seemed to be able to take her.

One night, as I was washing her in the bath, I told her to sit properly, as it appeared that she was not sitting straight. One foot reached the bottom side of the tub, and the other was a good couple of inches short of touching the white porcelain. She was unable to adjust, and I realized that she was indeed sitting straight and that her left leg was actually shorter than her right. With all the will in the world, she had learned to walk fully compensating for this anomaly, without the hint of a limp.

My wife and I were shocked. We took her to our family doctor the next day and learned that she had been born with a congenital dislocation of the left hip, or in common parlance, a "clicky hip," which should have been detected at birth. The most common way of fixing the problem, if caught early, was the use of double-thickness diapers, which would cause the pliable young bones to self-adjust to the correct placement. The doctor explained that her original socket had closed and the repositioned bone had formed another socket above the original one.

At the age of three, Sara went through a series of three awful surgeries over a nine-month period. The first entailed opening her side and exposing the hip, scraping out the original socket, dislodging the thigh bone from the secondary newly created socket, and pinning it into position in the original socket. Achieving the best angle required cutting through the muscle of the left thigh to expose the thigh bone, breaking that bone, and thus rotating the rest of the leg to an unnatural and grotesque angle. The surgical team would have to repeat the same process two more times before the problem was corrected.

Over the course of that year I spent hours at the hospital, where I felt so forlorn, so useless, so inadequate and incapable of helping my daughter in her anguish. Even when I put my hands over my ears, Sara's screams still penetrated my brain and provoked my totally unwarranted yet instinctive desire to rip the hospital staff to pieces. Logically, of course, I knew they were doing their best to help her, but it was still an overwhelming struggle for me.

At bad moments in my life, I can still hear her crying out in pain and terror. The thought of being around dreadfully ill children whose suffering I was powerless to alleviate was too much for me. The approach to the ward brought it all back. Although over a decade had passed, the memory was all too raw at the time.

It was difficult to speak of it to Whitney, but she listened to me carefully, then held my arm. She told me she understood, and that she would go into the ward without me as she did not believe she would be in danger under the circumstances. I can still easily recall the relief I felt at that moment when she spared me the pain of reliving my traumatic ordeal.

That's who she was. That care and understanding she gave to others is what should have been returned to her when she so needed help. I believe it could have made a difference.

We ended up skipping the planned concert in Taiwan, and on November 14, after close to a month touring Australia, we flew to Hong Kong for the final leg of the Far East tour. I was preparing for a show in advance and working at my hotel room desk in the Regent when Robyn burst into my room.

"David, come quickly! Whitney's lost her tooth!"

I ran into the bathroom, where I found Whitney holding her hand over her mouth and looking like the world had just come to an end. As she was brushing her teeth, her front tooth had come loose and gone down the plughole of the sink. I called hotel reception and had an engineer take apart the piping, hoping the tooth was caught in the U-bend. It wasn't.

Until then I did not know that Whitney's front teeth were all porcelain caps. She'd just won an America's Greatest Smiles award from the American Dental Hygienists' Association, and we had a show to do that evening, but with one front tooth missing, that would absolutely not happen. The mayhem such a cancellation would cause would render all that had been achieved during the Far East tour a disaster. Concerts in Hawaii and Taiwan had already been canceled in recognition of the overambitious schedule, and exhaustion was setting in. So Hong Kong was the last show of the entire tour. Never was there a time when the adage "the show must go on" had greater significance.

After several frenzied phone calls, and very much relying on our local hotel representative, we found a dentist specializing in cosmetic surgery who was able to replace Whitney's cap with a temporary one, understanding that she would need to go to her own dentist on returning to the United States. We were good to go, and everyone breathed a sigh of relief.

That evening Whitney was singing and thrilling the crowd, as usual. Near the end of the show, she turned to her backup singers to join them in a medley of Anita Baker's "Sweet Love," Janet Jackson's "Control," and Luther Vandross's "Stop to Love," a special extra for the last performance. Singer Billy Baker pointed at Whitney and then to his mouth, looking frantic. I saw it and my heart stopped. What had he seen that I had missed? Whitney immediately caught on, believing her temporary cap had fallen out. She reacted in pure shock, but like the performer she was, didn't lose a beat.

She covered her mouth with the microphone and carried on singing. I could see her run her tongue over her top tooth to confirm the loss of the temporary cap. At the end of the number, everyone started cracking up. Whitney had already realized Billy had played a joke on her, and she too joined in the laughing. Being the last concert of a long tour, everyone was a bit punchy and ready to relax and get home. Heaven alone knows what the audience thought—perhaps that the entire band had just lost its collective mind.

From there Whitney carried on, finishing the night with "I Wanna Dance with Somebody." In my estimation, the joke played on her actually made the performance better. It touched her sense of playfulness and confirmed a connection with loved ones, something she thrived on. Whitney had the entire audience on their feet, hands in the air clapping to the rhythm and singing along as she held her mic out to them. We were all lost in a wash of bouncing beat layered under the spine-tingling, joyous resonance that came from her throat. The backup singers came out front to dance with her, grinning at one another as they grooved and harmonized effortlessly. Whitney and Billy twirled and shimmied, buoyed by their shared joke as the audience, energized and captivated, "shared the heat" with them.

―――――――――

Whitney had performed 151 concerts in sixteen months, and the Moment of Truth World Tour was over. All were invited for a final party in her hotel suite. Every member of the tour group—hairdressers, singers, dancers, wardrobe, makeup, roadies—was there, and each received a "thank-you" envelope from Whitney stuffed with anywhere from $1,000 to $10,000. I alone didn't get one.

Michael Houston noticed and pointed it out to Whitney.

"No, David is going to get something else!" Whitney responded with a wink.

The envelope money was of no real consequence to me. Michael didn't know that as a vendor I was paid significantly more than the rest of the staff, and a bonus on top of that would have been inappropriate. I had almost concluded what I considered an extraordinary journey and an experience of a lifetime with all expenses paid and first-class treatment. I was somewhat saddened by the imminent end to it all.

Later in the evening and as the festivities continued, I was leaning against the balcony overlooking the Hong Kong harbor, taking in a tapestry of rainbow-lit skyscrapers whose reflection floated over the gleaming water. I sensed at first a presence and then a familiar figure at my side. An arm slipped into mine. It was Whitney. She looked relaxed and happy, and as stunningly beautiful as I had ever seen her. We both looked out across the twinkling bay. She nuzzled in and apologized for the absence of an envelope. I told her that there was not enough money to account for what I had experienced and enjoyed, especially in keeping her safe. Her playful demeanor changed, and she looked at me seriously.

"I will see you again, won't I?"

I left her in no doubt that I would be, and forever remain, at her beck and call. That moment had more value to me than any cash-stuffed envelope ever could. And yes, in that moment, I would have given up everything to change the role from professional to personal. She looked at me, smiled, and hugged my arm even tighter. We left the balcony and went back in to join the rest.

The party over, with all locked down and secured for the night, and with an early departure for the group to fly back to the United States in the morning, I retired to my room and lay on the bed. So much was going on in my head that I was unable to sleep. That has always been my curse, to the extent that I seldom sleep for more than three hours a night. As I lay there reflecting on all I'd experienced over the preceding months, I heard a noise outside my room. I rose and approached the door and saw that some Post-it notes had been pushed under it. I leaned down and picked up three handwritten notes.

One was from Robyn: THANKS DAVID, FOR EVERYTHING, BLESS YOU AND YOUR FAMILY. Well, that was a turnaround.

The other two were written by Whitney. One said, DAVID, YOU ARE THE BEST! LOVE YA ALWAYS. WHITNEY, and on the other, THANK YOU FOR ALL. I SHALL NOT FORGET YOU! WHITNEY.

My heart thumped hard as I was filled with pride at the idea that of all those she knew, at that moment, she considered me "the best." I wondered if she knew I had been a heartbeat away from crossing that perilous line to a place from which no one can return.

5

Mariah Who?

The next morning, I took Whitney and her entourage to the airport and bade them a safe flight with the appropriate number of hugs and kisses. By this time, I had learned that Americans are very physical with their salutations and seldom let a simple handshake suffice. And then they were gone. Feeling sadness tinged with expectation for the future, I waited at the airport for the required thirty minutes to ensure the flight did not return for any cause. I then returned to the hotel, completing my own procedures for the journey back to London that evening.

Once home I collated the memorabilia and framed certain pieces that could be used to impress visitors to my office at Premier House, Edgware. The two notes from Whitney were more personal, so I placed them in a single frame, which I kept near my desk so that I could glance, smile, and remember. Business at Churchill was booming, with executive protection assignments around the city and deep surveillance underway in Italy and the south of France, where our client required that his target be followed covertly as he crossed borders for various meetings. My team of former military surveillance specialists was keeping track of who this fellow met with.

Everything had run like clockwork in my extended absence, making me feel somewhat redundant. My management style has always been to effectively manage myself out of a job. I truly had some of the best operatives available, and they were mainly responsible for elevating the corporation from kitchen-table in 1984 to the third-largest company of its kind in the UK by 1989. It went from an initial annual turnover of £25,000 to £1.3 million in just five years.

But as always, not everything was rosy. My second marriage had finally run its course, having been on its last legs for some time. I cannot deny that this one failed in direct consequence of my infidelity—just as my first marriage (to my daughter's mum) had. Around this same time, my business partner, John Kingsley, and I had a falling-out. This resulted in the severance of our relationship for quite some years thereafter, but it has since been resolved.

I maintained sporadic contact with Whitney's friend Robyn and tour director Roy, mainly making recommendations about the fan club security and ways to identify the crazies before they manifested in physical form. A couple of months later I received a message from John Houston to contact him. He told me that Whitney had bought a home in a wealthy area of New Jersey and intended to hold her twenty-sixth birthday party there, with a proposed guest list of some 750 people, a no-expense-spared affair. John wanted me to perform a dual role on this occasion: come and survey, report, and recommend on what security deficiencies existed and needed to be addressed on the property; and prepare and set up the necessary security for the party. John was not at all happy, suspecting that both electronic and physical security was lacking, exposing the property and its occupants to all manner of vulnerabilities. Being expert in such matters, having carried out weekly checks on select London residences and embassies as part of my responsibilities as a sergeant in the Diplomatic Protection Department, I agreed. In late July 1989, I flew out to the States.

MARIAH WHO?   53

Whitney's home, known as North Gate, covered twelve thousand square feet and sat on five acres of wooded grounds. The modern design consisted of many interconnecting circular rooms, each one with curved floor-to-ceiling windows. I could see almost immediately that the newly installed security and fire alarm systems were utterly useless. It was patently obvious to me that Whitney had been ripped off. It amazed me that the contract alarm company was being called almost daily to attend to some problem. For example, the trembler alarms on the windows would activate when someone simply walked past them. The company employees had put plastic bags over the smoke detectors, because anyone smoking in the vicinity would set them off. I called in a US associate to evaluate the issues and provide an overview, suspecting this was going to be a disaster.

The entire system of security and fire-alarm equipment was valued at $3,500. Not only was it physically incapable of providing adequate coverage for a property of that size, but it was also a secondhand installation of outdated equipment. In essence, it had been ripped from another property and installed at Whitney Houston's. The system would have to be completely replaced. I was furious, and remonstrated with John Houston, demanding to know how he could possibly believe this piecemeal equipment was good enough for Whitney at her home. John was shocked, and immediately angry, knowing who was to blame. The Nippy Inc. accountants, Weidenbaum Ryder & Co., had recommended the installation company, which had promptly charged Nippy Inc. $150,000 for their professional expertise and skills, plus an onerous service contract. John did not really need me to tell him the charges were outrageous.

It turned out there was a pattern of excessive charging for all services acquired for the house, from air conditioning to swimming pool installation. Over a short period of time, Whitney and Nippy Inc. had lost hundreds of thousands of dollars to so-called professionals. Some theft could be proven; in other cases, it was simply suspected, but with good cause. John could no longer tolerate the corruption, and the accountants were removed. My work on identifying the irregularities cemented my relationship with John and caused other "professionals" serving the corporation to view my abilities in a slightly different light. I prepared a scathing report for John, and he acted promptly on my recommendations. The security and fire systems were upgraded immediately, and a system was installed incorporating perimeter fencing protected by a dual geophone network surrounding the property. Closed-circuit television installations completed the package initially, thereafter enhanced by a twenty-four-hour armed physical security team presence.

———————

Now that the security review had been completed, I had ten days to prepare for Whitney's massive birthday party. The local police in Mendham were fantastic, providing (at a fee, of course) a significant number of police officers, both off- and on-duty. Private security was provided by Garelick Security Services, a New York–based company renowned and skilled in high-profile events. I developed an enduring professional and personal rapport with its owners, Chuck Garelick and John Smaragdakis.

There was no shortage of celebrities in Whitney's life. I was told that for the previous few months, Whitney had been receiving bunches of roses from Robert De Niro. In this case, De Niro's attentions were considered by some an obsession as dangerous as any deranged stalker's. Not an individual used to taking no for an answer, he met his match in Whitney's mother, Cissy, who phoned De Niro and in no uncertain terms, as was her wont and style, told him to stop making a fool of himself and put an end to his obsessive behavior. He was not invited to the party. Whitney's beau Eddie Murphy would be there, and I looked forward to meeting him.

Despite the gargantuan security challenges, Whitney's twenty-sixth birthday party was enjoyed without disturbance. To me, it was somewhat embarrassing to see Eddie Murphy surrounded by his entourage of "bodyguards"—really just imposingly built men with no apparent skill set. I wasn't surprised. Many celebrities hire "big friends" with no practical security application know-how beyond being big, rude, and absolutely lacking in professionalism. That said, Murphy was, and remains, a natural comedian—as funny offstage as on. I liked him, notwithstanding his goons. Two years Whitney's senior, charming and handsome, and with a star power to equal hers, the Houston-Murphy relationship would have been a fine match. He appeared to me to be a straight-up, reliable guy.

For me, there were two events of relevance that night.

The first was the moment Whitney opened my gift. I had bought her a crystal paperweight in the form of a lion's head. Born in August, her sign in the zodiac was Leo and the animal held a special significance for her. Indeed, the logo for Nippy Inc. was a lioness. After opening my gift, she smiled and came over to me and said, "Thank you, David. Thank you for everything." There and then, she draped her long arms around my neck and kissed me, full on the mouth. A real kiss.

It was so unexpected. So very public. Yet for those few seconds, it transported me elsewhere with her, privately and alone. And then it was over. British reticence and embarrassment took over and I was back to the status quo, the moment gone forever but etched indelibly in my memory.

The second was the arrival of a bus outside North Gate, from which three men alighted, one of whom was a young rapper by the name of Bobby Brown.

Bobby turned up sporting a turquoise-and-white floral-patterned shirt with matching shorts, white socks furled around his ankles, and black shiny loafers. With his signature lopsided hairdo, he came accompanied by his brother Tommy and his assistant James. They were on the list and granted access. Later in the evening, I saw him make some of the lewd moves on the dance floor that he does when he performs for his fans. I was disappointed when Whitney jived a little with him. She could have been a great dancer in her own right, according to Aunt Bae, who used to say she was just too lazy to do it. She could, and did, match his physical sexual innuendo in a manner that, at first glance, made one think the two could actually complement each other when dancing.

The party over, everything cleared, all people gone or otherwise secure, I returned to my hotel at the HQ Plaza in Morristown, New Jersey. The next day I returned to London.

Whitney spent most of the first half of 1990 in the recording studio, creating her third album, *I'm Your Baby Tonight*. For each album there is a world tour, and for each world tour there is a promotional pretour. This means traveling constantly from one country to the next for innumerable meetings, events, interviews, radio and TV appearances, gala dinners, and the like. I was hired on as CP and we were back on the road.

The pretour began on October 30 with a press conference in Munich. Eleven tables were set up with eight members of the press at each. Whitney was to spend twelve minutes at each table, answering questions for the press with various TV and radio personalities.

The usual banter and media grandstanding was taking place when one of the German reporters posed an unexpected and most dreadful question.

"Whitney, they say that Mariah Carey is the new you, and has a better range of voice than you. What do you say to that?"

The table went quiet. The room went quiet. The collective intake of breath was palpable. We all waited for her answer. Whitney looked down and appeared to reflect momentarily. She then raised her head, squinted at her interrogator, and answered.

"Mariah who?"

Whitney could kill with a glance. The room erupted into laughter and no such question was ever posed to her again. The answer had been a Whitney classic, the reporter quashed by two words, and on to the next interviewer. Whitney won the room and the hearts of all those present.

Whitney did more press interviews the next day with individual reporters from Sweden, Norway, Denmark, Belgium, Greece, Germany, Austria, Finland, France, Italy, and Spain. Already anointed the Queen of Pop, Whitney had a vast audience and following throughout Europe. Meanwhile, some of her Black fans in the United States had begun to consider her "too White." For this, she had been booed at the Soul Train Music Awards two years in a row, in 1988 and 1989. But she soldiered on and didn't let it stop her.

During the seventeen days of the promotional tour, we traveled as follows: Munich → London → Miami → London → Paris → London → Basel → Amsterdam → London → Rome → Madrid → London → New York, with a full schedule of appointments in each city. There were eight of us on that whirlwind tour, which satisfied her producers, publicists, and promoters, all of whom made a pretty penny on Whitney's success. At the end of that exhausting two weeks, I started to wonder whether the price of fame was one worth paying.

In March 1991 we shipped out to Japan to attend the American Music Awards Concert Series as part of the I'm Your Baby Tonight World Tour at the Yokohama Arena. It was good to be back in Tokyo reunited with our Japan team, and where everything was now familiar to me. Also attending the same awards concert was a host of artists that included Kenny Rogers, the Alfee, Cyndi Lauper, Steve Winwood, Donna Summer, Gloria Estefan, and of course, Bad Boy Bobby Brown.

My heart sank. By this time, according to Michael, Aunt Bae, and others, Whitney was having a loose, ongoing relationship with this character. It was not talked about much by her family and friends within my earshot, as I suspect they too were hoping it would all soon go away. On this occasion, it was effectively a forgone conclusion that there would be interaction between the two stars performing at the same event. My thoughts turned immediately to security. The question to consider was what form that interaction would take, where, when, and at what risk to the security program.

In the end, the challenge was not to security, but rather to Whitney's emotions, and her interaction with Bobby brought many to the fore. Whitney performed on March 14 and 15. Rather than flying back right away, we stayed on for Bobby's show on March 17. We went to visit him before he went on. Walking into the dressing room, we found Bobby with the mother of one of his children, the child also being present.

The woman's attitude toward Whitney was immediately hostile. I could only imagine the battle of emotions Whitney must have been experiencing at the time. But she was no pushover, and her responses were equally aggressive, although more controlled, mature, and professional, as she effectively dismissed the woman. This stance angered the woman even more, which became clear as she beseeched Bobby to do something to support her against the "bitch."

We rapidly left the dressing room and proceeded to the rear of the auditorium to watch the "bad boy" onstage. Before they began to sing, Bobby's group banded around him, each putting a hand on the shoulder of the man in front of him as they held their prayer circle. The hypocrisy of their preshow praying, as with our own entourage, never failed to amuse me. They prayed for forgiveness for their sins long and hard before getting onstage with each show, and then they would promptly go ahead and commit those sins all over again the minute they got offstage.

Bobby was into his songs, not my kind of music at all, but to each his own. The guy actually could sing and had his following. Whitney was bouncing along to the beat when spontaneously and without obvious cause, Bobby stopped his suggestive gyrations where he simulates making exaggerated sexual acts on some unseen woman on the stage floor. He stopped singing mid-stanza, shouted "Fuck it!" to the audience, slammed his microphone down on the stage, and walked off. He left his dancers midstride and clumsily unbalanced, with the music continuing briefly before petering out.

Whitney rushed us all around to the dressing room, where Bobby was having words with the same woman he had been with before the show. Clearly, her reaction to Whitney had affected his ability to perform onstage. At this point Whitney lost her poise completely. I had never seen her like that. She had to be held back from ripping the eyes out of the woman's head. I believe it took both Michael and Robyn together to physically drag her out of there.

We got back in the minivan with good ol' Yoshi at the wheel, and we just started cruising around. Whitney was distraught. Emotions in the vehicle ran rampant. I learned during the drive that John and Cissy's long and sometimes troubled union had ended. Whitney and Michael were heartbroken. Michael in particular had a very overt and deep love for both his mother and father. In the car, he sobbed unabashedly. Tears being infectious in nature, the entire entourage was soon weeping. Whitney appeared more angry than sad. I was unsure if her anger was caused more by her parents' separation or by Bobby and his paramour.

Adding to the grief at the breakdown of the parents' marriage was the issue of John having fallen for his Latin American maid, some fifty years his junior, with whom he now lived in a high-rise in Fort Lee. The main bitterness over the breakup was universally directed at the young maid. An easy target, she was deemed the main reason and cause, and therefore an eternal focus for Cissy in particular. For Nippy Inc. to continue to run as a partnership, a compromise was eventually and begrudgingly achieved with the stipulation that John would never bring this woman to any event where Cissy was present.

The Bobby Brown debacle, combined with the deeply troubling news about John and Cissy, cast a dark cloud over all as we made the journey back to the United States the next day. Whitney's star was still rising, and her career was yet to reach its zenith. But from my vantage point, that was when her course changed, when the fire within her slowly began to die.

6

The Lexington Incident

On January 17, 1991, the United States bombed Iraq and the first Gulf War began, ending sixteen years of peacetime in the United States. The country was unsettled, adjusting to the reality of young lives in danger overseas. Just ten days later, Whitney sang her iconic rendition of "The Star-Spangled Banner" at Super Bowl XXV in Tampa, Florida. True to her nature, and very much in response to the situation her country was in, she gave that song her entire heart and soul. Smiling wide as she sang, Whitney changed the timing of the piece and held the high note *free* longer than the usual, transforming the anthem into something all-encompassing, unforgettable, and yet to be equaled. Commentator Frank Gifford, who introduced her, described it as the most electric moment he had ever seen in sports. Once again, her soaring voice and magnanimous spirit opened and filled a space only Whitney knew we all carried in our hearts.

A few months later, she flew via helicopter to a battleship in Virginia to greet returning troops. Later that evening she held the Welcome Home Heroes concert, which was transmitted live to soldiers overseas from the naval air station in Norfolk, Virginia. She sang her heart out to thirty-five hundred servicemen and women returning from the Gulf War. HBO broadcast the concert to more than fifty-three million households.

Needless to say, when the United States and Canada leg of the I'm Your Baby Tonight World Tour commenced on April 18, 1991, the nation's love for Whitney had deepened exponentially and her fame had skyrocketed. I flew out to take charge of the tour security and prepare for the long road ahead. We would travel by bus for four months, nonstop, covering thirty-five thousand miles and seventy-eight separate venues, with a final show on August 17 in Ottawa, Ontario. Rather than taking a circular route, we crisscrossed the United States and ventured up to Canada several times. Specially designed coaches were commissioned for the tour. My home was to become a luxury armchair at the head of the bus along with Whitney, Aunt Bae, and Silvia, Whitney's personal assistant. Robyn and the rest of the women in the executive party would travel in the female dancers' coach.

The logistics for moving such a group in this manner were enormous, as were the supporting security operations. The schedule would be demanding, if not altogether punishing, but as we embarked on the journey, enthusiasm ran high among all the participants.

On April 19 we traveled from Tennessee to Lexington, Kentucky. We had a day off before a show scheduled for April 20, and the entire tour party was invited to a private club to watch the Evander Holyfield versus George Foreman match. "The Battle of the Ages" was an incredible fight by two exceptional boxers that culminated with Holyfield walking away the victor.

We returned to the hotel, happy and cheerful from the evening's get-together. While walking to our rooms from the elevator, we passed the concierge area on our floor, and I noticed three young men in the lounge eating and drinking. I positioned myself between Whitney and the eyes of these males. We were approaching Whitney's room when I heard a scream behind me. It was Aunt Bae.

"David! David!" she cried. "They're beating Michael."

I rushed over to find Michael Houston lying on his back on the floor of the lounge with the biggest of the men, a three-hundred-pounder, lying across his lower body, holding him down. The fittest, most muscular was kneeling on his chest and punching him repeatedly in the face and head. The third bloke, the little one, was standing on the sidelines, cheering on his friends. Michael was struggling but trapped. Aunt Bae was screaming and attempting to pull the fat one off Michael's legs.

At that point, I saw red. I flew at the guy who was pummeling Michael's face. I'd always defended the underdog and hated bullying of any type. I delivered a classic uppercut (one that Holyfield would surely have appreciated) that literally lifted the man off his feet, snapping his head and upper body in the opposite direction of where he had been positioned. That single blow propelled him over a sofa onto a marble table beyond, where he then rolled onto the floor. He arose shakily.

His face was a bloody mess, his forehead opened, a gash stretching from the center of it around his right eye and halfway down his cheek. He attempted to stem the flow of blood pouring between his fingers. As I continued to approach him, he held out his free hand to fend me off, crying, "No more, no more, please!"

By now the fat one was standing, as Aunt Bae and Michael had succeeded in removing him from Michael's legs. I turned and put my face in front of him to challenge him, then pushed him backward. At that moment I felt a massive blow to the back of my head. A full bottle of beer had been smashed on top of it and blood and beer were dripping everywhere.

I turned to find the short one immediately behind me, looking terrified. Clearly, this little runt had grown a pair of big brass ones somewhere in the past few seconds, but by the look on his face, they were rapidly shrinking back to peanuts.

I grabbed him by his shirt and raised him off the ground. He started screeching, "It wasn't me. It wasn't me!" As I constricted his throat to almost beyond the point where he could speak, he squealed, "I didn't do it," and pointed toward where Whitney stood in the lounge corridor. Over his shoulder, on the other side of the table that contained the Heineken bottles, I saw Whitney standing transfixed, her beautiful eyes the size of saucers, with both hands over her mouth. She moved her hands and I saw her mouth, "I'm sorry! It was me!"

I realized instantly what had happened. In the heat of the battle, in an effort to protect her brother, Whitney had picked up the beer bottle from the table and had thrown it, aiming for the fat guy. I had inadvertently put my head in front of his, thus shielding him from getting a full-on hit to the face. Had the bottle blinded him, I'm sure he would have sued for many thousands if not millions of dollars.

I threw the little chap aside, disgusted and still very, very pissed off. I turned and all three raised their hands in submission. They had received enough and withdrew sheepishly, yet quickly, for fear of my pursuing them. In my Welsh rage, I was not happy with the ease of their submission. I so wanted to finish them off. But my priority was to remove the principal from the scene and out of any personal danger.

This I did, moving Whitney, Michael, Bae, and Silvia into Whitney's suite. I was bleeding badly, as head wounds tend to do, and my right hand had started to swell. It was already close to twice its normal size. While Silvia, ever reliable and ready to help, went to get some towels, Whitney grabbed me and hugged me hard. She tended to me in a frenzy, shocked at what had just taken place.

"I'm sorry. I'm so sorry!" she cried, tears pouring down her cheeks.

I assured her that hitting me with the bottle was a better outcome than having smashed Michael's attacker with it. Whitney was torn between tears and laughter. I usually retain a wicked sense of humor even in adversity, so before long, laughter was the new order of the day in the room. Her hugs got bigger and closer—and very, very much appreciated by me. In fact, at that precise time and while the clinging embraces endured, I felt no pain at all. Go figure.

What only Michael and Bae knew at the time was that Whitney had been the initial target of the three men's racist verbal abuse. As she, Robyn, Silvia, and I had walked ahead with Michael and Bae in the rear, dawdling as they spoke and joked together, the men had accosted Michael.

"Hey, n—. How's your nappy-headed n— sister?"

Michael, the staunchest defender of his sister and undoubtedly not a stranger to rabid racial discrimination, lost it and rushed them head-on. He was built like an athletic dynamo, so how the three of them had floored him was beyond me. Alas, they had—and now his face showed the marks of this miserable and cowardly three-on-one beating.

The news spread rapidly, and before long members of the group came up to the suite. Gary Garland, Whitney's half-brother, was very angry and barely able to contain it. I was secretly glad he hadn't been there and could only imagine the three rednecks would have likewise been extremely grateful they had missed him. I didn't know how far Gary would go once he started: He was big, strong, and full of pent-up rage. I might not have been able to stop him when in full swing and operating in defense of family. We now had a potential media catastrophe to contend with. I broke away from the suite and phoned Whitney's father John and attorney Sheldon, and then sat down and typed out my report and statement covering the incident, swollen hand and all. I declined treatment from the emergency services personnel. I knew I had to move fast so the lawyers and their team could start the ball rolling.

I accepted full and unequivocal responsibility for the injuries I caused in the skirmish, as I had done so solely to protect Michael from further assault. The police were involved and took reports. I was happy with my actions, knowing that they would withstand the strictest judicial scrutiny. I looked forward to the day in court when I could expose the bigotry of the three perpetrators.

Sadly, it was not to be. Nippy Inc. settled out of court. The bastards got a no-fault award of $150,000 for the assault on them. It turned out that my single punch resulted in twenty-four stitches for my "victim." The price of paying was far cheaper than the price of the publicity that frenzied media attention would have brought. Put simply, the potential damage to the brand just wasn't worth the risk.

The incident made the press but was quickly forgotten. I sometimes wonder whether that idiot looks in the mirror, fingering the scar over his eye and across his forehead, and thinks of that night, and how being a bigoted bully awarded him that badge of cowardice.

———————

After that incident, while the wound on the back of my head was healing and we were traveling in the night after shows, Whitney would sit directly behind me on the bench chair and part my hair at the injury site to see how it was healing. Without stitches and scabbing up, it would take some time. The attention was gentle and kind, and again much appreciated.

There was a cozy, familial feel to our tour bus now. Bae did the cooking in the onboard kitchen, and tour members would line up outside Whitney's bus to wait for her famous homestyle meals. She knew precisely what Whitney, who was a picky eater, liked and would actually eat. Chicken, mashed potatoes, collard greens, biscuits, and gravy. She certainly needed regular sustenance to deal with the grueling nature of travel and the emotional drain of show after show. Bae was her mom away from home, so to speak.

When not being fed by Bae, and with what came to be my living dread on the road, Whitney had an overwhelming obsession with the 24/7 restaurant chain Denny's. The food was good, cheap, fast, and there was plenty of it—especially if calories and heart attacks were not a concern. It's a place where at any time of the day or night, and particularly along the extended stretches of American heartland roads, the whole group could enjoy hearty fare. At 3:00 AM it was no novelty to hear Whitney call from the rear of the coach to pull in. She fancied a snack and had seen the sign in the distance, so our coach and any coach traveling in tandem with us would stop and "take over" the restaurant.

Michael Houston was grateful for my intervention in what had become known among us as the Lexington Incident. He was very protective of his sister and always carried an element of guilt regarding an accident with a coat hanger that reportedly nearly ripped out Whitney's voice box during some game they were playing when they were children. The two siblings shared an intense love for each other. During their childhood Cissy was always on the road, a gap filled by John and Bae, as well as other family members. Apparently not all those experiences were good. It has since been alleged that one of those other family members subjected the children to some elements of sexual abuse.

Difficult familial experiences were never spoken of. The feeling was, if you don't talk about it, it didn't happen. I nevertheless witnessed a love of family that had eluded me during my own childhood. Whitney's family loved her completely, and she them. Troubles and all, it was a privilege to be accepted as a part of the family, though obviously to a lesser degree.

My mother died when I was eleven and my sister was three. Before my mum succumbed to her disease, she was treated for many months in Clatterbridge Hospital, a cancer treatment center outside Liverpool. I visited her there and clung to her horribly ravaged form. She was sent home to die, having lost all her hair. She showed me her massive scar leading from the front of one shoulder around and across her back to the opposite hip, along with the purple-colored markings and crosses indelibly printed on her upper body that had been used to direct and guide the radiation beams.

Despite her weakness, I was so happy to have her back home. Alas, it was a short-lived visit as she was removed to Stanley Hospital in

Holyhead, and I never saw her again. I did bicycle there to give my father a plastic rain hat that had arrived as a free gift in one of the woman's magazines she subscribed to, so that she could keep her head dry when she came out of the hospital. But she never did.

I remember the day my father drew the curtains in the parlor, the custom when an occupant of the house had died. He sat me on the sofa and cried as he told me that my mother had gone to heaven, where she would no longer be in pain. I had never seen my father cry before.

A year and three weeks after her death, my father married the nurse who had allegedly been holding my mother's hand when she died— or so he told me. Upon reflection, I think he said that to establish a maternal connection between the two women in the hope that I could more readily identify with my stepmother, regardless of whether it was true. That was never to happen. To me, she was everything bad about the stepmother jokes. She was cold and selfish and never accepted me for who I was.

And I never accepted her as a replacement for my mother. She tried to mold me into her idea of a good son, which made me feel inadequate and resentful. My father banished my maternal grandmother, who was living with us at the time, when my grandmother tried to stop my father from beating me because I could not work out some arithmetic homework. After Gran left our house, I had no contact with my mother's side of the family until much later in life.

It was not uncommon for my father to use his fists on me as I troubled my way through being a teenager without a mother or a consistent group of friends. He served as a police officer and moved us from place to place every eighteen months as he proceeded through the ranks. In those days, no police officer in Wales could serve more than three years at any one location—a strategy for avoiding the potential for corruption through bribery, as well as the possibility of becoming too familiar with the environment and subjects to be policed and losing their impartiality.

I attended five different schools in my educational career before I left home at the age of fifteen. After a move, when I started a new senior school, my stepmother sent me to school wearing shorts. To my utter embarrassment, I was the only person of my age there so attired. It is hard enough to assimilate into a new school environment at the best of times. She just made it immeasurably harder. I had learned to use my fists and realized that by taking on the bullies for the underdogs, I could earn respect. Not love, of course, but something I could live with as an acceptable substitute.

My stepmother was an Irish Catholic, and in her eyes, if you were not a Catholic, you were a lesser being. The way I saw it, that view in itself—that some people are lesser than others—goes against the teachings of the very Bible she held up above all else. Her hypocritical Catholicism was her substitute for real human emotions. I saw similarities between her and Cissy Houston. I guess you could say I equated Cissy with my stepmother, and Aunt Bae with the mother I lost. Cissy was heavily involved in her Baptist church in Newark, where she was the choirmaster. When she sang gospel, it was as if the angels had stopped breathing to give her all the oxygen she needed to woo them. She had an incredibly powerful voice. But her attitude of superiority, her grasping need for control and attention, reminded me of what I had endured with my stepmother.

On our long trips across the United States, I spent many hours talking with Aunt Bae. She was tormented by the loss of her missing older daughter. I made her a promise that I would use my US investigative contacts, of which I had many, to try to find her missing child. Although I was able to procure the help of US investigators with significant prowess and access to specialist data and information, they failed to turn up any trace of the child. The most plausible conclusion is that she must be dead, and possibly had died without her identity being known, or in circumstances where no real effort was made to establish the origins of the corpse.

While she was disappointed in the failings of her daughters, Aunt Bae nevertheless held no boundary or limit to her love for them. In contrast, my father only once told me he loved me, and that was because I asked him directly as he lay on his deathbed. At my father's funeral in October 2008, Hefyn, an extremely tough and incomparably skilled detective both feared and revered on the streets of Caernarfon in Wales, told me something I hadn't known. The pain-delivering street brawler, a personal friend and longtime fighting partner of my father, said to me, "You have no idea how proud your father was of all you've achieved. He talked about you all the time."

I looked at him and was unsure whether he saw my pain. I replied, "You're right, Hefyn. I've no idea. He never told me, and now it's too late."

My father came from an era when men did not cry or express any weakness traditionally associated with women's emotions, such as love. As a result of all this, I tell my daughter every time we talk, "I love you."

I witnessed a different kind of parenting as I grew close to Aunt Bae that summer. The maternal care, protection, and acceptance she expressed for her daughters and showered on Whitney brushed off a little onto me. It was a warm feeling I had yearned for from the day my mother passed. You never know where you may find something you've lost.

7

Dueling Threats

As the summer wore on, Bobby Brown started making his presence felt on the tour. Whitney seemed overjoyed. It was obvious her feelings for this character ran deep. For me and the rest of those who were close to Whitney, it was a dark day and the start of an era.

We all knew of Bobby's unfortunate reputation. Cissy hated him for it, and she told Whitney not to marry him. But that directive was precisely what provided the extra push for Whitney to seal the deal. There was no way Whitney was going to allow Cissy total control over her personal life. It created a familial rift that affected everyone. Indeed, Bobby's increasing influence over Whitney, coupled with the heartbreak associated with the deteriorated marriage of John and Cissy, was arguably responsible for the demise of the original Nippy Inc. operation.

I was prepared initially to put down all the hype around Bobby's "bad boy" image as fake or, at least, exaggerated media coverage. I did not judge him. I felt I had no such entitlement as we came from such different backgrounds. Renowned for his misogynistic behavior and violence, he surrounded himself with several hulking, intimidating security men who became known as "bookends." They were actually nice guys by themselves, but Bobby often created trouble that they had to resolve on his behalf. It was said that he had been selling drugs from the age of ten on the street corners of Boston. He owed thousands to dealers and gang leaders, which Whitney was reportedly obliged to pay.

In choosing and pursuing this relationship, Whitney gave me cause to doubt my hitherto self-proclaimed ability to discern a person's character effectively on sight. Sadly, no one but Whitney wanted him there. As the relationship and his presence grew, it became obvious that he could not rise to the level of Whitney's talent or intellect, nor that of her musicians and tour personnel, so she made the conscious decision to lower her own standards to make him feel comfortable when he was with us. At first I presumed that Bobby was a passing infatuation. Nothing else made any sense. The fleeting sexual thrill of the "bad boy" syndrome. A short-lived straying off-track to spite her mother. Eventually, she'd turn to someone who was a better match for her. To my incredulity, it did not happen.

That summer we showed in Atlanta, where we stayed at the Ritz-Carlton hotel in the Peachtree district, the same neighborhood where Bobby had his mansion. I spent a couple of uncomfortable hours at the mansion, waiting for Bobby and Whitney to finish whatever it was they were doing in his bedroom, ever mindful of being the only White person there. My presence was tolerated because Whitney said so, but, I felt, only begrudgingly so.

Bobby's residence was a stately edifice with a large tin gold-painted silhouette of a bowler hat, his trademark, and the big initials "BBB" displayed on the gates. Outside, bare-chested security giants were playing basketball. On the inside it was a veritable village and an ever-rolling party. Two dozen people apparently lived there—relatives, friends, hangers-on, girlfriends, wives, other people's girlfriends and wives, children, other people's children—all there with the same intent: to exploit the situation for their own needs for as long as it lasted and until they were thrown out. Strangely enough, some of that crowd ultimately ended up on Whitney's payroll, as did most of Bobby's family. It was James, Bobby's always-embattled, abused, and misused personal assistant, who, feeling for my isolation within the crowd, kept close to me. With him, I was able to communicate and have a reasonable conversation, as he didn't introduce the word *motherfucker* into every other syllable he uttered.

During the tour Bobby floated in and out of our lives like a bad smell. He brought in a new era of excess, mainly alcohol related. Michael and Gary appeared to accept him more readily than most other family members or staff, and I had no doubt that was related to Bobby's familiarity with drugs, booze, women, and partying. This new level of debauchery was not anything that I was overtly aware of initially, but it manifested instinctively as a feeling, a worry, a developing concern.

Bobby Brown was not the only disruption to the 1991 American tour. It was, of course, not without its "devoted fan" incidents. Three weeks into the tour, on May 7, as we arrived at the Pacific Coliseum in Vancouver for that evening's concert, Robyn handed me a letter and a card. They were handwritten in neat and mature handwriting, but the content revealed a rather sick and dangerously enfeebled mind. It was not signed, but Robyn was of the opinion that it came from a known "fan," HAROLD WALKER, who regularly communicated with Nippy Inc. and who often sent correspondence and packages via Federal Express, as this letter and card had arrived. She had checked with Maria Padula, a staff member involved with Whitney's fan club at the Fort Lee, New Jersey, office, and was able to confirm her suspicions. It would indeed appear we were dealing with the same individual. I was advised that there was a long history of communications by "Harry" with the office.

I was then informed that Whitney had been made aware of the letters and their contents and, to my absolute horror, she'd intimated her desire to call this man up to the stage when she was performing. Oblivious to what I saw as clear red flags in his letters, Robyn must have convinced Whitney that it was a good idea to make what she considered merely an enthusiastic fan a part of the show. I vehemently argued against any such proposal, having a completely different read on the letter. Thankfully, Whitney agreed not to take an active part in any interaction with this character. Considering the subtext of the content of the letters, which betrayed an obsessive personality, I was certain this was the best course of action to adopt. I asked Tony Bulluck, the tour manager, to allocate a security guard for our bus when it arrived an hour ahead of the show to protect Aunt Bae, who would be cooking her usual meal for Whitney on the coach. Whitney's tour bus often attracted more than desired levels of attention.

As always, Tony's response was immediate and a guard was quickly allocated to the task. I proceeded to the stage area and briefed the venue security personnel, alerting them to my specific expectations and the need for additional vigilance. I instructed them that under no circumstances was any person to approach the stage area. They would have to look to me to discern which were genuine fans wishing to hand over flowers or other tokens of appreciation.

Harold Walker's letter included the detail that he had "counted the days for a month" in anticipation of the event on May 7. From that, we concluded that he must have purchased one of the very first tickets. I looked to the promoters for some feedback as to what seating an initial purchaser would be able to select for the event. Tony's highly able assistant, Norman Williams, advised on the process of ticket sales at this venue, and it was clear that Walker would be in front of the stage. Beyond that, all we knew was that it was unlikely he would be seated any closer than eleven rows from the front. In the end we got that part wrong.

I concentrated on viewing the public on the floor level in front of the stage, but could not, at that time, determine the presence of anyone suffering from the digestion of "wild mushrooms," which was one of the ways Walker had indicated he would be getting up the courage to "meet with Whitney." Surveillance of the attendees was maintained as the seats started to fill and during the opening performance by the supporting group After 7. We then noted some empty seats in the area to the front of the stage. Having delivered Whitney onstage for the commencement of her performance, I took up the usual position to the immediate front left of the stage.

As soon as Whitney began to sing, I noticed a man, who turned out to be Walker, taking a seat up front on the aisle corner of stage left. This seat was empty during the opening act and did not become occupied until the house lights were extinguished in anticipation of Whitney's entrance onstage. It was by this clandestine means that Walker had avoided obvious detection and seemed to appear out of nowhere. It was planned and executed rather well, actually. He was dressed in a pair of jeans, white shirt, and cowboy boots. His estimated age was mid- to late thirties. He sported a mustache and had long, graying hair that flowed over his shoulders, the front part of his forehead accentuated by gradual male-pattern baldness. His eyes, which were very large and bulbous, created the impression of a permanent state of shock or horror.

When Whitney began to sing, Walker began breathing deeply, effectively in gasps, as if hyperventilating. He undid the top button of his jeans and pulled at the fly, allowing greater access for his hand, which he inserted and appeared to commence masturbating, all the while staring frantically at the stage. He then began repeatedly mouthing the words *I love you*. Letting go of his genitals, he quickly bent down and promptly pulled off his boots and socks and then started to undo his shirt buttons.

I signaled to the venue security personnel, and those closest to Walker approached him. He stopped his undressing routine. To my horror, the venue security staff elected to let him remain and "keep an eye" on him as they decided what steps should be taken—a remarkable delay to what to me should have been an immediate and forcible ejection of the sick man from the premises.

Walker was still seated with no change in his wild and demented expressions, but he was now shouting about the worship of Satan and Lucifer (still referring to Whitney). Clearly, the situation was not going to improve, and the female attendee unfortunate enough to be seated next to him was now obviously distressed at his antics. Realizing the security at this venue would not make a move without a supervisor's approval, I caught the eye of their team leader. In sign language, I left no doubt that the lunatic needed to go. Once they were given the authority they needed, not another second was wasted in removing Walker, though one had to return to recover the items of clothing he had removed and discarded. Walker was ejected from the building and never seen nor heard from again.

The entire incident was over in moments, before Whitney had even started her second song of the evening. Whitney was not at all aware of the potential scene that was brewing just a few steps away from her. But after the show and when on the bus, we all talked and had a good laugh about it.

———————————

Due to the persistence of these types of deranged fans, we developed a program with the official fan club staff operating out of the corporate office in Fort Lee and headed by Roy Barnes, the tour director. There were more than fifty people on our watch list. I retained files on them all. Many believed they were married to Whitney. Others were sure they wanted to be married to her. The women generally followed themes of hatred and wanting to "cut her," or cause some other form of extreme harm, often involving removal of body parts.

Several declared they were her twin sister and had decided this was the time to reunite, either hating or forgiving Cissy Houston for her cruelty toward them by separating the sisters at birth.

Many troubled individuals did not focus only on Whitney. Family members and staff were often included as possible targets. One man sent a plethora of communications to Robyn, Cissy, and Whitney, including the delusion that Whitney had given birth to their son, "Little Charlie." He had taken his aberrations to the New Hope Baptist Church in Newark, where he revealed to Reverend Charles Thomas the details of a plot wherein Cissy was involved with Eddie Murphy to kill Robyn Crawford. He assured the pastor, "Yes, Whitney and I are lovers. Yes, Whitney and I have a baby." He then showed the reverend a signed and notarized document naming Robyn and Whitney primary and contingent beneficiaries of his group life insurance policy.

In another instance, I arranged to meet with a violently motivated character in a local car park. There he was surrounded by police officers in the recreational vehicle he lived in. He had been following our tour itinerary and was seen on location at several of our tour venues across the country. Within the vehicle, the police located illegal firearms, knives, and detailed plans of venues, residences, and properties, including a youth camp in upstate New York owned, operated, and often attended by Mariah Carey. He planned to visit and kidnap her once he had dealt with Whitney. There were also two pit bulls in the vehicle—fighting animals, ears cut to the skull and teeth sharpened to points.

Dealing with all the machinations of twisted, sick, and deviant minds means living with a constant and consistent level of threat that never totally goes away. It can be deferred, it can be stalled, but never minimized, overlooked, or forgotten. The moment you let down your guard is the moment they will strike—they only have to get it right once, I have to get it right all the time.

––––––––––––

The threats from unknowns are an even greater challenge because there is no advance warning. This is where a skilled and ever-alert team is of the utmost importance. We learned this lesson on July 26 in New Jersey. During the late evening following a successful show at the Meadowlands Arena, I escorted Whitney back to her dressing room, as I usually did. However, on this occasion, the usual routine was complicated by the presence of a film crew engaged in recording materials for the video scheduled to accompany the release of the new song "My Name Is Not Susan." My usual policy of prohibiting admittance to a sensitive area by anyone other than "qualified laminate holders" had been defeated. The security-versus-publicity battle was never-ending, and security seldom won.

There were several entities filming that were not associated with the promotional video team; we were dealing with multiple dubiously vetted individuals and had been doing so for the duration of that very long day. The corridor was full of working personnel and their equipment. For the filming, Whitney had proceeded from the stage past her dressing room door, which, due to the filming of the music video, then bore the nameplate SUSAN.

We were required to return to the dressing room through the crowds, which, with a fine display for the cameras, Whitney accomplished with her usual aplomb. On entering the dressing room, a man dressed in a white suit approached from behind and tried to seize her. I believe that neither Whitney nor Michael, who was at her side, was aware of his proximity at the time. I grabbed the perpetrator before any contact was made and, in handing him to another venue security guard, saw him ushered quickly up the corridor and away from the dressing room area. It was established that he had no official pass or other form of authority to be where he was, and he had merely joined the crowd leaving the stage area after the performance. He was detected and no longer posed any threat, but such was the tenuous nature of the environment that night.

Once Whitney was safely inside, I left the task of guarding her dressing room in the competent hands of GAYLE WRIGHT, my security assistant at the time. She was a former Norfolk police officer who had been with us since the beginning of the tour. Wiry and slim, yet muscularly built, with short blonde hair, she did well initially and assimilated quickly into our security team, an alien working environment for her. Very discreet and professional, her application toward her duties was flawless. Gayle traveled on another tour bus but always provided additional cover for me on the floors of our respective hotels.

Life for security personnel on the road is very hard. It is draining and exhausting, with little sleep or opportunity for quality rest, and no stand-down time expected or provided. A constant high level of vigilance is required, which other personnel could happily abandon once a show was over each evening. Security was, by definition and demand, perpetual. It takes a certain type of individual to maintain a high and consistent level of performance over protracted time frames.

Believing Gayle more than capable, I attempted to locate the male interloper and security guard to interview them both in the hopes of identifying the hole in our backstage protocols. However, the interloper had already been removed and was not available for questioning. On returning to the hallway, I was walking toward the dressing room area from a distance in excess of forty feet when I saw a man wearing a LOCAL STAFF maroon T-shirt approach the dressing room door. Understanding that the door bore the name SUSAN and not WHITNEY, I was aware that in such a hectic environment, innocent errors could be made. But so could meaningful acts of malicious intent.

To my complete horror, the man grasped the handle as if to enter. I screamed a warning to Gayle, who was less than four feet from this intruder, as I burst toward the door. Everyone in the corridor stopped what they were doing. All movement ceased, even that of the male, now in the process of entering Whitney's room. Gayle was standing there, totally distracted and oblivious to the man's actions. As I arrived, I grabbed and yanked him backward. Unfortunately, Whitney was already there at the door, confronting the man herself.

Whitney could not have been more pissed off, and justifiably so. Especially with me! It was my responsibility to make sure no one entered her room. In the same amount of time it had taken me to run forty feet, Gayle had only managed to stand up from where she was seated on an equipment packing case. Her lack of response made her of no security benefit whatsoever. She could have reached out and grabbed the idiot, as she had been less than four feet away at the time. To my surprise, her attitude was not one of remorse for the gross dereliction of duty but rather "What's all the fuss about?" It was clear that for whatever reason, she had lost the flow, was off message, and could no longer work or operate at the level demanded. It was time for Gayle to go.

I met with Tony to review the security personnel situation and find a replacement for Gayle. On July 30 it was decided that we would be joined by Wayne "Smitty" Smith, my next security assistant. Whitney was happy. She knew and liked Smitty because he had previously toured with none other than Bobby Brown.

The hiring of Smitty was the beginning of our two worlds colliding and interlocking. When Bobby was present with his boisterous behavior, he drew unwanted attention and crowds in circumstances where we otherwise would have passed unnoticed. This, of course, made more work for me. While his presence caused disruption, his absence was sometimes even worse when he escaped to "do his thing."

As we toured in the Midwest that summer, on one occasion Whitney was to perform at an open-air concert. The opening act was about to proceed onstage when Whitney telephoned Bobby at his hotel room in Atlanta. A woman answered. Everything stopped. Management, promoters, insurers, and sponsors held their breath. Whitney was beyond distraught, which was becoming typical under such circumstances, the upshot being she canceled the show.

Arthur Singer, our intrepid travel agent from New York, arranged an immediate flight to Atlanta. As crowds were still pouring into the arena, Whitney, her assistant Silvia, and I were driving to a local airport where a private jet was already on the tarmac, hired to the tune of $15,000, waiting to fly us to Atlanta so that Whitney could confront her beau about his apparent infidelity.

It was a sobering moment for me. Why would anyone lucky enough to have this beautiful superstar, so totally and obviously in love and committed to him, ever bother to look elsewhere? (I eventually came to believe Bobby had an addictive personality. Beyond alcohol and narcotics, based on the level and consistency of his infidelity, it certainly seemed some form of sexual addiction was at play.) And what the hell kind of lack of professionalism was at play in this picture, where the star of a show could leave the venue while concert attendees' money was still being collected for an event the promoters then knew was not going to happen?

Could Bobby really mean so much to Whitney that she would risk sacrificing her reputation, her career, her everything for him? Why didn't she just tell him, through whichever tart had picked up the phone, to screw himself and the horse he rode in on, and be relieved of the ever-escalating emotional burden? How the hell had Bobby taken this dominant female artist, loved by millions and with the brightest future imaginable, and rendered her a veritable emotional cripple? Could it be the embarrassment of having to endure her mother, above all others, waiting in line to say "I told you so?" What logical reasoning could there be for what was taking place? For the life of me I could not come to terms with what was happening before my very eyes.

I think it boils down to the possibility that some people simply take the abuse regardless of their status and station in life. It was difficult to watch. It reminded me of my days as a sergeant at the Harrow Road police station, where the wives would line up *again* at the station desk on a Saturday night with bloodied faces, eyes hanging on cheeks and noses flattened, wanting their husbands arrested *again* for beating them up *again*. And then by Sunday, those same women would be back pleading with me to not have their husbands charged *again*, because they loved the assholes and had forgiven them *again*. A recurrence extremely sad to witness but a very real syndrome, and clearly one not restricted by class, wealth, color, creed, or religion. Managing this threat was well outside the scope of my limited psychology skills. Just give me a terrorist or a crazed fan and I'm in control.

We landed in Atlanta, where a limousine awaited, engine running, and then we were at the Ritz-Carlton, zooming up the elevator to the floor where Bobby was staying. I half hoped he had vacated the building, but he had not, and he let Whitney into the room. Silvia and I waited outside, still not daring to breathe or think too much. Some form of heated discussion was taking place, and I was wondering whether to send Silvia for a second key. But then new sounds emanated from within, and it was clear they had reconciled their differences, the bedsprings and accompanying moans and groans cluing us in. Unbelievable.

—————————

The tour progressed west. In Los Angeles, we stayed at the Peninsula Hotel in Beverly Hills. By coincidence, Bobby happened to be staying at a cheaper hotel in the area. I remain uncertain whether there had been another issue of compromise that Whitney had detected but, sure enough, we were on our way to his hotel, and with attitude. Arriving there, we found Bobby's room was on the ground floor, a corner room with corridors running along the front and side. Whitney acknowledged the presence of Bobby's crew lounging about, and one of them told her where his room was. The crew watched open-mouthed and anticipating the worst, as there was no way they could warn Bobby. As she approached the door to his room and started slamming it with her hands, I turned around and Bobby's crew had vanished. Something was clearly wrong, and if they could not fix it for him, they did not want to be a part of it.

Whitney started kicking the door and screaming Bobby's name, all seemingly to no avail. Could it be that he was not in the room, contrary to what the crew said? Some movement at a fire exit door attracted my attention. Silvia and I quickly went down the corridor and looked through the glass door to see a woman in a state of near undress being held under the arms by a pair of strong brown hands and lowered from Bobby's window into the garden below. Her clothes followed hurriedly thereafter. If it was not so damned ridiculous, the scene would have been hilarious. There was an unspoken understanding between Silvia and me that she would be the one to tell Whitney, a burden I was glad not to carry.

At this point, Whitney was bringing the house down at the door to the room, almost literally. I suspected hotel staff would soon appear, or worse, other residents with cameras, which would be fatal to her reputation—not that she gave a damn about her reputation at that moment. The girl was on fire. Thankfully, and probably after sufficient time to support his story on this occasion and by so rearranging the inside to corroborate, the door opened and a bleary-eyed Bobby stood there in his underwear, looking as if he was completely at a loss to understand what was happening as he had been so soundly asleep. At two in the afternoon. *Yeah. Right.* But in short order, the unmistakable sounds of passion came from the room. This debacle ended identically to the one in Atlanta, aside from the throwing of a woman out the window (which was just as well since Bobby's room in Atlanta was on an upper floor).

―――――――――

Near the end of the tour, Whitney, Robyn, Silvia, and I were at an Applebee's, one of Whitney's favorite restaurants, on a day off from the touring regimen. The meal over, Robyn and Silvia went to do their thing and I was left in the near-empty restaurant with Whitney seated across the table from me. We were chatting in general when she abruptly stopped. I immediately looked around, thinking she had seen something that had caused her concern, such as an approaching fan, but no such threat existed. Looking earnest, she reached across the table and grabbed my wrist.

"David, I wanted you to be one of the first to know and ask you. I'm going to marry Bobby. What do you think?"

The first thing I thought went something like: *You are fucking kidding me, right, boss? This is some form of joke, right? You have completely lost your mind. You're not well, you need rest!*

In the nanoseconds it took to process the news and assess and dismiss a host of negative responses, I hoped she'd interpreted my expression of total disbelief and absolute shock as one of excitement and anticipation for her. I responded to what was clearly a fait accompli, "Wow! That's news, boss. You are a lioness and, like all lionesses, you will look after your cubs regardless, and Bobby will be one of them."

She smiled, pleased with the response from a confidant.

"Yes, I will," she said proudly.

I realized that I had, in her mind, just given her affirmation that she was making the right decision. I would live to regret it, as ultimately would she. But I knew she would have to endure significant criticism from family and friends in the immediate future. I let her have her moment. I suspect it was very much what she wanted to hear and desperately needed to feel. I would not deny her that feeling of happiness, no matter how utterly incomprehensible the mere thought of such a union was to me.

By now, I realized that Bobby's reputation was not something just crafted for the sake of a professional persona, or even unjustly glorified by the press. It was precisely who he was. I was sorry for her, but it was an important moment in her life and I, with my own deplorable history of failed marriages, was the least qualified person to give her advice. Conversely, I may have been the best person to do so. But it would have shattered her.

I chose the easy option.

8

Make It Happen

The European leg of the I'm Your Baby Tonight World Tour
began in London. Between September 1 and 15, Whitney did
eleven shows at Wembley. My daughter, Sara, then eighteen and
studying for a biology degree at Cardiff University in South Wales,
traveled to London with her boyfriend to see Whitney's show. I had
not seen her in over a year.

After the concert they came to the hotel, where I introduced them
to Whitney and Bobby. Whitney was charming, giggling and laughing with her, asking questions and making jokes with regard to "her
father," which Sara loved. I could not help feeling uncomfortable
watching what I interpreted as Bobby, in true lecherous form, appearing to undress my daughter with his eyes. When he invited her to
stay for drinks at the bar, that was it. I took Sara and her boyfriend
to their car, and they were on their way back to Wales. That was not
going to happen on my watch.

Whitney later told me she thought my daughter was beautiful,
which indeed she is.

Because Bobby Brown was with us in London, our time there was
not without incident. Near the end of the stint, I received a frantic

telephone call at about 5:00 AM from one of my drivers. He was agitated, babbling, and difficult to understand. Once he calmed down a bit, he told me that Bobby had come to him after hours without my knowledge and made him pick up Whitney's brother Michael and take them both to Browns nightclub. He went on to say that Michael and Bobby had been fist-fighting on the banks of the Thames and that the police were on the scene separating them at that very moment. He feared they were going to be arrested, which is a course of action I surely would have undertaken without a second thought, back when I was a police officer, regardless of how important such idiots believed themselves to be.

I could hear some screaming and shouting going on through the car phone. My driver told me that he had heard Bobby encouraging Michael to return to the club to rob a drug dealer working there, whose acquaintance they had made during the evening. This plot apparently did not sit well with Michael, who promptly refused and, in physically trying to keep Bobby in the limousine, they struggled and then burst out and carried on fighting in the street. Bobby's argument was that the dealer in question had a briefcase full of money and cocaine, and that such a person would never report the robbery to the police. Bobby was out for money and drugs, and Michael was not going for it, out of respect for his sister. Michael may have been a rascal, but he was definitely not a thief.

My driver was able to convince one of the officers to come to the car phone. I asked if the officer could please refrain from arresting them and instead get them back to the hotel. The officers accepted an apology from me as a former Metropolitan Police sergeant, agreed to my request, and unceremoniously threw Bobby and Michael back in the limousine. I was hopeful that the officers would treat this as a nonevent as a favor to "Sarge" and that it would not make the morning papers.

Michael was taken back to his hotel. Bobby returned to the Conrad, where he stormed past me into the suite. He had taken a well-delivered slap or two, but it must have really irked him to know that I knew of his antics. I did not broach the incident with Whitney, but I did tell her father. And nothing was ever said again. The chauffeur was experienced and discreet enough to realize any loose lips on his part would likely end what had the makings of a very lucrative client relationship.

Issues of this sort were increasing due to Bobby's near-constant, invariably belligerent, and seldom sober presence. Every two days, Tony, the tour manager, was sending Bobby a crate of Heineken and a bottle of Courvoisier, delivering it directly to Whitney's suite. On the third day, Bobby would be inactive and ill, getting over what must have been close to alcohol poisoning. The problem was that Whitney was trying to keep up with him, and this was negatively affecting her health. This was the start of the rot that was to ultimately condemn her to an early grave.

Before leaving London, someone thought it would be a great idea to have a farewell soiree. I was consulted on the venue and advised that a club by the name of the Valbonne was under consideration. I had some strong reservations about this plan. The traffic situation alone at the Valbonne would expose Whitney considerably. I suggested that the Bootleggers nightclub, then run by my friend Gary Van Praagh, was preferable from a security perspective. It was very close to the hotel, so Whitney could effectively step out of the vehicle and, in just a couple of steps, be across the footpath and into the club. Any lurking photographers would be kept at a distance. The intimate environment would be conducive to enjoyment without compromising on safety.

However, behind my back, an Arista organizer made an advance visit to the Hippodrome nightclub in Soho, and to my horror, I was advised that it had been selected. Back in 1988 I had categorically identified the Hippodrome as one the most ill-advised locations for Whitney to visit. My opinion was based on local knowledge, for which there is no substitute in my profession, and on my time as a policeman there. But no one was listening to me. I was told that the event was technically being organized by Arista, Whitney's record label, and our local sponsors. I was shown a letter wherein the Arista organizer had rejected Bootleggers, claiming that the club did not have a late-night liquor license. This was absolute nonsense, as I had arranged for the organizer to communicate directly with Gary at Bootleggers, and in fact a license had been extended to 2:00 AM. Later, I was able to confirm there had been no contact whatsoever by any Arista individual with the club. Put simply, the Arista organizer lied.

I received a telephone call from an individual named Danny, who said he was responsible for Hippodrome security. Apparently someone from Arista had told him that I had given my assent for this venue selection. I told him I had not, and never would—that I was wholly against my principal attending that environment, and even more so on this occasion as Bobby Brown would be present. Danny assured me there would be no members of the press present, and there would be no prepublicity regarding this event. Having no alternative, I was left with the task of trying to make it work however I could.

We were promised that the side entrance would be permanently manned for ease of access to the establishment. When we arrived, it wasn't. We were left knocking on the door like beggars seeking scraps. I sent a security officer inside to secure the facility and get the damned door open while the principal's vehicle was obliged to travel on a rerouted journey to return when the door was manned and ready for us. On our return, we were given every indication that access was now available, and we again entered the side street. However, the staff in the club failed to respond. Whitney and a highly wound-up Bobby were both annoyed by the delays, one's angst feeding the other.

She stated that she would forget about entering through the side and instead walk through the melee at the main entrance. After all, "This is why I have security, isn't it?"

We were then obliged to walk some sixty yards through a mass of paparazzi, all of whom had been invited by tour promoter LINDA NEWMAN—something I was never made aware of in advance, of course. Naively, I had expected only a few passersby going back and forth between Leicester Square and the entrance to the Tube at this "non-publicized and very discreet affair" on a Sunday afternoon.

On leaving the club some four hours later, we were again greeted by the paparazzi, now even more determined and aggressively disposed. As a result, there was much physical contact between our moving party and those seeking to reach Whitney, in the form of pushing, elbowing, and more than a little stomping on insteps. My team and I had no choice but to fall back on our street cop ways. I gave a short, sharp elbow in the solar plexus to a random person in the crowd. This brought the recipient to their knees, creating a block against those pushing from behind to fall over, forming a still bigger barrier to surmount while we made our getaway. This classic move was a beautiful thing to see and an absolute joy to execute, being one honed through many years of policing violent demonstrations and rowdy football fans.

The British public woke the next morning to press coverage that was, as always, exaggerated to ill effect, and with little or no reference to the truth. All the good publicity Whitney had received before that night was forgotten. This disaster was attributable to the total lack of communication between various agencies at every level. I found and lambasted Linda for lying and for her self-serving manipulation to the detriment of my principal. I was unmoved by her self-indulgent tears, which were a cover for her singular bad judgment.

There were those who sought to identify my security personnel as unprofessional and culpable. That was absolutely unacceptable to me. My principal wished for us to take her through the proverbial gates of hell. We did so, and we kept her safe. I placed the blame wholly on those who willfully, and for reasons of some form of self-enrichment, elected to ignore the best professional advice available at the expense of her safety. I submitted my report to Whitney's father, John, as an anticipatory means of defending my own position, and more important that of my staff.

As I wrote in my report, had I been guilty of some form of dereliction of duty, I would have been the first to say so. I am not, nor was I ever, infallible. I have always recognized that with the best will in the world, I too make mistakes. There are three former wives who would readily attest to that fact. Had I made any mistakes that night in the context of executive protection, the consequences would have been far more serious than bad press. Potentially tragic.

———————

Whitney's saxophonist, Kirk "the Bishop" Whalum, was one of the most sincere and profoundly Christian men I have ever had the pleasure of meeting and befriending. He officiated the prayer circle before each show and held group Bible studies that Whitney occasionally attended when we were on the road. At the end of that tour, in Spain, I decided to try it out. I entered the meeting room with Whitney and Robyn and joined the circle. As we held hands, various attendees started making noises—undecipherable, but ominous-sounding to me, and somewhat unnerving as the crescendo grew and grew. I linked the two hands I was holding together and backed out of the room, never to return for a repeat exposure to whatever the hell was going on inside those meetings.

I was told that the congregation had been so moved by the prayer and the presence of their Lord, they had started speaking in tongues. Damn! I am unsure whether it was the frenzied gibberish being mumbled and shouted or the fact that the noisemakers appeared to understand and respond to each other in a language of nonsensical word strings and utterances that bewildered me the most. In any case, after that one attempt, I chose to stay outside the door of any room where the "service" was being held, leaving them to it on the inside. Both Whitney and Robyn were highly amused at my discomfort, which of course I magnified for effect.

From London we had traveled to Amsterdam, Munich, Paris, and finally A Coruña, Spain. Next up: the filming of *The Bodyguard* with costar Kevin Costner. This being Whitney's first film, there was much excitement and buzz. Behind-the-scenes preparations were already in progress as we toured Europe. I was advised that a walled and gated property was being rented in Beverly Hills for Whitney and entourage to stay at during the scheduled five-month project, with a carriage house on the grounds to accommodate me. I was very much looking forward to this new experience.

I was in the lobby of our hotel in Paris when I was approached by Toni Chambers, the new executive vice president and chief operating officer of Nippy Inc. Somehow Toni managed to be both a friend and confidant to Cissy Houston and was considered John Houston's ears and eyes on the road in his absence. She had been drafted to our tour and immediately thrown headlong into the domestic dysfunction and conflict that always simmered between John and Cissy. She was also seen by many as being a plant sent to usurp the authority and control that Robyn Crawford had over Whitney. It was difficult to discern her loyalties, and the scene was set for many clashes.

Toni took me aside and told me that I would not be going to California with Whitney to make the film. I felt like I had been clubbed in the stomach with a nine-pound hammer. I eventually recovered somewhat from my utter shock and disbelief, along with a rapidly rising temper and, as appropriately as I could muster, inquired as to the reason why. Toni said that they were taking Smitty, my security assistant, because the role expected of him was more in keeping with a typical security guard, of whom expectations were limited, rather than a professional personal protection officer. What? How was anyone to make sense of this statement? I was disgusted and immediately asked if Whitney knew. Toni said that she did and was in agreement. She even gave the impression that it was Whitney's decision. I looked over to where Aunt Bae was seated. She looked back at me in silence, tears in her eyes. She knew. Robyn cast a sly glance in our direction, feigning innocence. She was guilty.

I was gutted. Feeling used and unappreciated, I considered quitting on the spot. I had to take a second look at the closeness I had come to feel with the whole group. Where, exactly, did I stand? I decided to wait and see what John had to say before making any decisions.

The next day, as we were preparing to leave Paris, a troubled John asked to speak with me outside on the steps to the St. James Hotel. He apologized, claiming it was not his idea at all, and that this was the brainchild of Toni, supported by Robyn and Bobby Brown. They had all persuaded the group that having a White trained professional bodyguard on staff was a little too close to the plot of the movie, and might spur the public to speculate on how much truth there was to the fiction. More specifically, they had determined that my presence could somehow overshadow Whitney as the "focus" of the film, or that I may have become involved in consulting or advising for the venture.

Where the hell did they come up with this nonsense?

John assured me that this was a "fluid" situation, and in any event he would be bringing me back after the film to resume where I had left off. My ire dissipated, as I felt sorry for John. I could see the steps being taken by Cissy and her supporters to neutralize his effectiveness and involvement with Whitney. My loyalty to him and his daughter was sacrosanct and could not be compromised or leveraged. I realized he was in an untenable position, and I subsequently wrote him a letter to further lessen his burdens in my regard and to keep all doors open.

———————

Within two months, in late November 1991, John got in touch with me. He was troubled by several issues on both a personal and a corporate level. At home he was worried about the activities of his new wife, a beautiful young woman who apparently was giving John cause to question her fidelity. At work, the business had become a "split-camps" affair, which affected everyone professionally as much as it did personally. From the penthouse apartment on the Englewood Cliffs where John and his new bride resided, there was almost a direct line of sight looking north along the Hudson to the office in Fort Lee. John wanted to know what was going on both at his office and in his home when he wasn't there.

Despite his incredibly loyal personal staff, John still felt he was being kept in the dark about certain things. Both his driver, Farouk, and Roy Barnes, his right-hand man, gave him information. And to a certain extent, Aunt Bae did as well. John and Bae had historic familial ties, but she was often conflicted because of her loyalties to both Whitney and Cissy. Bae was, in many respects, the glue that kept the family from totally falling apart, especially on the road while touring. Roy was developing medical issues that were adversely affecting his ability to travel and even continue with regular day-to-day operations. Sadly, within a few short years, Roy passed.

When John reached out to me, I responded with my corporate mantra and adage from inception, "The answer is yes. What's the question?" He knew I had contacts through which I could acquire covert equipment, precursors to the now highly popular devices that report all manner of data from a cell phone or computer. At his request, I was able to acquire two devices. They were installed at both locations, his home and his office, the task being simplicity itself. All that was needed was brief unrestricted access to the two telephone units concerned.

The equipment sent a signal to remotely record any sounds from the lines for recovery at will thereafter. Being powered directly from the telephone lines, the only batteries needed were for the recorder in the event it had to be used without access to an electrical socket. John was now able to listen to anything said on either of those two lines. After the equipment installation, he appeared to acquire a peace of mind that had previously eluded him.

Once the task was completed, he and I never again discussed the matter beyond a nudge and a knowing wink. John understood that knowledge and information translate into power. It was my opinion that the power he wielded was utilized to good effect against all comers. There must have been many who wondered how the hell John kept one step ahead of them. I knew.

———————

Shortly thereafter I relocated permanently to New Jersey. The company I had engaged to install security at Whitney's house back in 1989 had reached out and offered me a position as management consultant. Churchill had disintegrated, as had my second marriage, and I was ready to leave London. I needed a new direction and decided to take the plunge.

On January 2, 1992, I boarded a plane at Heathrow, and I was gone. Gone from the land I had served to the best of my ability in so many different and varying capacities for so many years, seemingly to no avail. With trepidation and excitement, I questioned what on earth I was doing—a Welsh boy from a rural farming community leaving my country to travel to another one on the other side of the world to start the second half of my life. *Hell*, I thought, *people have been doing the selfsame thing, under substantially more trying and difficult circumstances, for centuries.*

John Houston was good to his word, and I was soon working on security enhancements at Whitney's residence in Mendham in preparation for Whitney and Bobby's July 18 wedding. While it was anticipated with joy by Whitney, the rest of the family could hardly pretend to understand her. We all hung on to the possibility and hope that in the next three months she would see the light and call it off.

Michael's wife, Donna Houston, was the lead for the event, supervising the complicated logistics. She was a proficient and skilled no-nonsense woman, perfect for the job. When up against any hitch or snag thrown our way, she'd say, "David, we just have to make it happen." And we did.

We had hoped to keep the event under wraps as much as possible, but even at that early stage, the media believed they already knew all the details about the wedding and its guest list. They spouted forth with conjecture and speculation, which then became fact to them, and no doubt countless readers and listeners. The event date and location were being published, with radio stations like Philadelphia's Star 104.5 repeating and embellishing the information every time they played one of Whitney's songs. From my security perspective, I needed to know what media coverage was to be permitted. Which celebrities were being invited? What form of identification would the legitimate press be required to wear? Would there be advance media involvement, and would they have access to the residence and grounds? What would be the rules for taking photographs? Would the event be televised? How soon could I receive a guest list?

And what of the fans, old and newly enraged? The news of Whitney's nuptials had caused an onslaught of angry fan mail, from males mostly, but not exclusively. Many felt so completely let down, cheated, and abandoned that they becameforlorn and embittered. The injury and hurt any number of emotionally displaced fans wanted to inflict upon Bobby was an eye-opener in itself, but he had his own security personnel to look after those threats. The potential for any one of these unfortunate beings to show up in person on the big day was a major factor that could not be ignored.

We got to work and started to make it happen. A couple of fields were rented from a local farmer to park the vehicles that were expected to accompany a guest list of more than six hundred people. Garelick Security Services (GSS) of New York and the Mendham Township Police were engaged for security. A major concern was the potential for the use of narcotics by guests. Discretion was requested: for example, not dragging someone across the wedding venue for smoking a joint. A delicate balance and potential "temporary blindness" were the order of the day for law enforcement. Very much a fingers-crossed situation for all.

The uniformed officers were to handle traffic control outside the property. The wedding ceremony was scheduled for 2:00 PM, with a sit-down celebratory dinner, under canvas, at 6:00 PM. That would be followed by entertainment, expected to conclude at about midnight in deference to the fact that the happy couple were due to embark on their honeymoon on the Concorde from JFK International Airport early the next morning. Michael and Donna were to accompany them. No security was being taken on the honeymoon. Michael was covering, as it was anticipated it would be a low-key vacation out of the spotlight. *Yeah, right.* From what I'd seen, Bobby Brown didn't do "low-key." I suspected a more emotional reason for leaving security behind but said nothing.

No members of the media were to be permitted inside the premises. Should any arrive, they were to be penned and monitored by GSS personnel throughout the event. There would be one professional photography company on the property, a team of seven individuals who would take and develop photos on-site before departing. No attending guest, including all staff and vendors, was permitted to have or use a camera or video. Any attempt to bring such equipment on the property would be denied and the guest given the option to leave their camera with the GSS staff manning a security post externally or go home. Thankfully, this was in an age before cell phones.

The day arrived and all was going well, but Bobby had not turned up at the appointed time for the ceremony. The Brown family had been bussed in from Boston and were occupying the top two concierge floors of the HQ Plaza Hotel in Morristown. It was there that the groom spent the night before the wedding. There had been some hard partying going on—very hard—and to our embarrassment, reports were received that the two floors had been trashed. Whitney's Mercedes sports car was likewise trashed. She had loaned it to Bobby's brother, Tommy. He returned it filthy, with foot marks on the white lambskin ceiling and the seats slashed. As I recall, there was between $5,000 and $10,000 worth of damage to the upholstery and interior alone.

A search party was sent out, and Bobby was eventually brought to the property from wherever they found him in Morristown. He was properly attired and at least present in body, if not in spirit or soul. The ceremony was officiated by the oldest of the Winans brothers, a wonderful pastor from a family of renowned musicians and famous gospel singers.

And so, sometime after the originally scheduled hour, Ms. Whitney Elizabeth Houston of Newark married Mr. Robert Barisford Brown of Boston, and the deed was done.

On to the reception. From a security perspective, it was an astounding success with all entities integrating well and working as a team throughout the long day. Twenty-four would-be trespassers were hindered from attempting to scale the property fences. An unauthorized and extremely low-flying helicopter sought to compromise the event briefly but flew so low the craft's identification was easily observable, and GSS placed a complaint with the Federal Aviation Administration. GSS had anticipated intrusion by air and had arranged for blimps to be tethered and flown above the property. The press and media representatives who turned up were successfully penned and caged, creating a palpable degree of frustration, chagrin, and angst in them, but no one really cared too much about that. They would write whatever they wanted to invent the next day anyway.

Donna's brother, Darren, was responsible for security within the residence itself, but he decided to go home without telling anyone. I was called to deal with an incident where a waiter had been caught inside, roaming around unsupervised. He claimed he had been directed by an unknown woman to enter and bus glasses. When I arrived where this kid had been detained in the garage, now substituting as a bar, his story proved false: it was clear he carried no tray or other receptacle for bussing glasses. We searched him and found nothing of an incriminating nature. Reportedly the son of a police chief, the boy had obviously been helping himself to alcohol. He was summarily dismissed by his manager and escorted from the premises.

One guest ran up to the married couple, produced a camera, and snapped a photograph of them before running off and trying to leave the property. When caught, he denied possession of a camera. However, a search of his pockets revealed the truth. The camera was destroyed, and upon questioning, he admitted that he was paid one hundred dollars by the person who acquired his pass to the wedding in return for a promise that any proceeds from a published photograph would be shared.

The DJ, having sneaked a camera in with his equipment, was also seen discreetly taking photos of the married couple. His camera was confiscated. Upon seizing a camera from a third individual, we were instructed to return it, as apparently Whitney and Bobby had given this person permission to take a picture. We had no choice but to acquiesce. An unfortunate precedent set, the private photography situation degenerated rapidly and guests were allowed to take pictures freely, creating conflicts with the official photographers. The picture-taking should not have been tolerated, but to take the appropriate action would have caused severe embarrassment. It was a bitter pill for the team to swallow, and it did taint the evening somewhat from our perspective. But when the joyous occasion finally came to an end, on balance, we had won the day.

The groggy, burnt-out, barely sober honeymoon party left the reception at 3:00 AM and ended up missing the scheduled Concorde flight. I remained on property with the GSS staff, and we jokingly discussed retaining the event plans for the divorce party that would surely follow within the year.

9

Zenith

The latter half of 1992 was taken up with wrapping up the filming of *The Bodyguard*, which meant Whitney was busy recording soundtracks and preparing for not only the movie's release but also a 730-day world tour that would follow immediately.

Work began in San Diego and Las Vegas for the period of September 24 through October 5. For the Vegas shows we stayed at what were once the private suites of Frank Sinatra at the MGM Grand. The penthouse had a circular design, with rooms leading off from a vast central space. I was housed in one of the conjoined rooms, controlling access within. We had two shows there, with a day off in between. During that down day, while everyone in the executive party was relaxing or sleeping, Robyn came into my room. She handed me a cassette and told me to listen to it. I put the cassette in my player and pressed play. Holy God above. The haunting acapella beginning, the crystal-clear lyrics, the message being expressed. Heaven had arrived here on earth. There is Welsh choral music that in its melodious melancholy can tear a heart asunder, and this song immediately did likewise. It was Whitney singing "I Will Always Love You."

The song was written and originally sung by the famous and ever-enduring country singer Dolly Parton. Whitney had interpreted it with the most bewitching, soulful arrangement I had ever heard. I was stunned. I could not move. The song ended, and I played it again, and again, and again, digesting every word, every meaning, every feeling. And then I was overcome by an urgent need to speak to Whitney—not something I often initiated other than in emergency circumstances, preferring her to take the lead on any casual rapport.

She was in her room, in PJs and a robe, relaxing and listening to music through her earphones. Whitney had a wonderful fragrance about her, a mixture of baby powder and Keri moisturizing cream. I still use that cream to this day, having been introduced to it by Whitney, and the innocence and purity of that aroma being comforting. She looked up, not terribly surprised and perhaps expecting my visit as she knew what I had been doing, and she was aware of my love for music. Her style of music in particular.

She took off her earphones and smiled. "What do you think, David?" How could I possibly deliver as many words as I wanted to without making an utter idiot of myself? I gathered my senses. "Boss, this is the best song I have ever heard in my life." I could actually feel my eyes welling up. Damn! I was about to make a fool of myself.

She smiled and said, "Thank you."

"No, thank *you*." I nodded, turned, and I think I floated back to my room.

————————

A few days later Whitney shot the music video for "I Will Always Love You." As we walked back to the limousine that afternoon immediately following the shoot, she grasped my arm.

"David. I have something I would like to tell you."

I stopped, quizzical, as this was unusual. With a smile that earned her international acclaim for its beauty, she looked at me and said, "I'm pregnant!"

A host of emotions assailed me from every direction, the most prominent being happiness. Hers. Yes, this was incredible news, and I think she identified with my excitement for and with her.

"Will it be a boy or a girl?"

"A girl!" She squeezed my arm still tighter.

"That is incredible, Whitney. I can assure you there is nothing like a daughter to make your life complete."

Two things here: First, I seldom referred to her directly by her first name, that feeling too informal for our relationship. I generally addressed her as "boss" or, on occasion, "Ms. Houston." Second, she knew I had a daughter and had met her. She could identify with the sincerity and meaning of my statement, knowing the love I have for my Sara. The moment was etched into our respective memory banks—well, mine at least—for all time to come.

Within seconds my mind turned to security. A thousand questions came flooding in. When, where, protection, travel, changes of protocols, who will the nanny be, schooling, local or boarding, and so on and so forth. The list of security protocols increases considerably when children are introduced into the mix. Just ask the members of the Royalty & Diplomatic Protection Department of the Metropolitan Police, dedicated to the protection of HRH the Queen and her children and grandchildren. Whitney was about to enter a whole new world of magic and wonder, and my workload would increase exponentially.

———————

The premiere of *The Bodyguard*, in all its anticipated glory, was held at Mann's Chinese Theatre on Hollywood Boulevard on the evening of November 23, 1992. After a very long day of security preparations, the event went without a hitch. That is, if one accepts organized chaos as the norm. Crowds from hell with cameras, press, and media were everywhere, like a plague. But we made it through, and Whitney and Bobby Brown were centrally seated in the theater. As the lights went down, I took a standing position to their rear with good viewing access. I would like to say I enjoyed the film, but I did not see the production fully until some days later, when I could attend the local cinema by myself and without distraction. The pregnancy brought with it certain needs that could not be denied, and Whitney required escorting back and forth to the restroom frequently, so the ability to even pretend to view and digest what was on the screen was not an option. At the time, and on the return to the hotel, I could not have told anyone how the film started and had no idea as to the content of the ending, as Whitney herself did not remain to the end. She was not feeling well.

We returned to the Peninsula, where a celebratory reception was being held. Whitney did not spend much time at the event. While there, one of the more prestigious magazines approached, seeking permission to interview me. John Houston and attorney Sheldon Platt were standing there together, and to my utter surprise, they gave a thumbs-up. So I was interviewed and photographed. The entire process left me wondering about the additional exposure such publicity would bring. Why now, after expending so much effort to avoid associating me with Whitney prior to and during the actual filming, was I being presented to the press? *This is the real bodyguard. This is the one being played by Kevin Costner.*

Whitney returned to New Jersey almost immediately after the premiere. The pregnancy was now becoming consuming, and at home with proximity to her doctor was certainly the best place for her. There were some three months to go before the birth, and her pregnancy was not an easy one, unfortunately.

I stayed in Los Angeles and took the opportunity to see the film in my own sweet time and without any work distractions. I ended up being quite shocked by the obvious similarities between the events in the film and those of my everyday reality. Take away the sex, scandal, and shooting, and one was left with much of what Whitney and I had experienced together in the past five years, condensed into two hours. The parallels were undeniable.

I too had tried to refuse the job when it was first proposed to me. I too had bought and listened to her music to better understand a potential client. To me it was just a natural thing to do in my quest to precisely understand the person I was to protect. I too had dealt with following vehicles and persistent fans. I too relied on contacts from previous posts to obtain important information. I too had to protect Whitney from obsessed fans and overzealous paparazzi. I too had been obliged to extricate Whitney from scenes of utter chaos, generally caused by the stupidity or greed of others. I too had navigated confrontations where the desire for publicity was at odds with my determination of security needs. I too had to interface with big guys who thought themselves bodyguards and believed incorrectly that they knew what they were doing. I too was appalled by the state of security at the principal's mansion, and helped to enhance it. I too was obliged to mutter, "I told you so," all too often. And the list goes on. There was even a scene where Whitney holds on to the back of Mr. Costner's sweater as she walks behind him, as she did many times with me when we traversed crowded environments.

I was immediately struck by the proverbial chicken-and-egg question. Was this the original script, written twenty-two years earlier for Steve McQueen to play the role of the bodyguard, with Diana Ross as his principal? At that time the events depicted in the film could never have been even a figment of a non–science fiction writer's most fervent imagination. Or was this a work adapted from the original script and manipulated to better represent the real life of Whitney and her bodyguard in the '90s? It was quite obvious, really. The original story had to have been altered to incorporate modern technology. It was written in an era when the protection discipline was employed mainly through thuggery by muscular goon types, knuckle-draggers with limited access to equipment, professional knowledge, training, or communication tools. No, the script had clearly been changed to include the technically enhanced security protocols of the '90s, and the storyline adapted to the actual life of the star playing the role of the star.

It was clear to me that Whitney was absolutely playing herself. She was very, very good at it, and the only deviation from our working and personal script was the inclusion of sex, shooting, and explosions, elements of the film that would have been developed as crowd-grabbing and thrilling fantasy. One practical downside, from my operational perspective, was that we had now forsaken any potential value in booking Whitney into hotel accommodations under the name of Rachel Marron. It is a certainty that the original scriptwriter had not serendipitously chosen the same name we had been using for years to hide her identity at hotels. That detail alone proves that Whitney and/or her people had a hand in modifying the script. What else was added based on her real life with me? The answer is certainly known to others, but well above my pay grade.

The Bodyguard grossed $411 million, and the soundtrack became and remains, some thirty years later, the bestselling soundtrack album of all time.

———————

And we moved on. That meant preparing for the birth of the little bundle who would become the light of Whitney's life in the form of Bobbi Kristina Brown. The pregnancy had not been an easy one. Whitney was carrying excess water, which caused her ankles to swell, making it difficult for her to walk. She was ultimately placed on some form of monitor, which automatically relayed data to her doctor for constant review, as long as she was near a fax machine. In late January 1993, as the pregnancy progressed and the swelling remained, Aunt Bae, Silvia, and I accompanied Whitney, by private jet, to Merv Griffin's home in the Bahamas.

It was a beautiful cottage on private grounds, serviced by its own staff and on the edge of a powder-white sandy shoreline, with palm trees, turquoise seas, and of course, the availability of a telephone fax line. A touch of heaven on earth to prepare for her impending miracle. No Robyn, no Bobby Brown (he was on tour at the time), no business machinations with which to contend, no press, no record producers, no paparazzi. Just idyllic peace and relaxation. At least as much as her condition would allow.

We spent days on the beach, swimming (actually, walking into and standing in the water) and watching the frolicking dolphins but a few feet away. Balmy breezes and fragrant tropical smells teased the senses as her bump and the bundle of joy within grew. Aunt Bae tended to Whitney as if she were a china doll, and with good cause, as I understood the incessant swelling during pregnancy could be dangerous. I was personally apprehensive about how the change of pressure in an aircraft could affect Whitney, but the obstetrician dismissed my worry.

There came a time when her doctor was sufficiently concerned by the readings he was analyzing that he suggested Whitney return for closer medical attention, should a need develop. The date of the birth approached, and our stint in paradise came to an end.

With the impending arrival of a baby in the United States comes the baby shower, an opportunity for relatives and friends to provide gifts of necessities and niceties, and just about everything in between, to the expectant mother. The event was held in private rooms at a

Manhattan hotel on February 20, 1993, with a host of names, personalities, songwriters, friends, associates, hangers-on, and the usual crowd of those who wanted to appear as if they were close and significant to Whitney. And what do such people buy one of the wealthiest mothers-to-be in the world to make it meaningful? Many beautiful and equally practical baby items, which left me pleasantly surprised.

As it was an exclusively female gathering, much of my time was spent out of earshot and out of sight. But judging by the excited laughter, there was little doubt a good time was had by all, especially Whitney. Of course, the event had been splendidly arranged and managed by Donna Houston, and I used the opportunity to begin planting the seed of the need for enhanced 24/7 home and child security, shortly to become a very pressing consideration.

As we entered March, we went into a controlled panic mode. I moved into the Hilton opposite St. Barnabas Hospital in Short Hills, New Jersey, and set up operations from there. Once again working with Chuck and John of Garelick Security Services in New York, and supplemented by Major Security Services, the hospital's security company, we moved to close down, protect, and secure every environment where Whitney might be in the hospital beyond the private room she was allocated. We had been instructed specifically not to allow any living person an opportunity to photograph the baby once she was born.

The moment nearing, Whitney was moved into her room on the sixth floor of the maternity unit with twenty-four-hour security on all access points. The floor had been swept and secured, the fire exits and all other points of potential compromise manned and patrolled. The doctors expressed concern over some unspecified developments with the pregnancy and decided on a cesarean delivery. On the morning of March 4 the lead doctor asked me what time would be best for the cesarean from a security perspective. We agreed on 11:30 AM for various reasons—morning visitor rush over, people focusing on lunch, a natural lull period in a nonemergency environment—and we were ready to go.

As I recall, Bobby missed the actual birth. He turned up having already been celebrating and suitably oiled, leaving shortly thereafter to continue partying with his people. For him, such an event was not new, of course.

Bobbi Kristina Brown was here at last, and in perfect condition.

As she had with Whitney herself, an emotional and overjoyed Aunt Bae was one of the first to hold the little scrap of humanity and welcome her into the world. At the time I believed the emotions to be joy, but retrospectively, they could have been expressions of trepidation. Bae was very intuitive and insightful—she could read Whitney like a book.

The baby's tiny footprints were taken for identification protocol purposes. I was surprised when standing there with Bae, as the baby had a very pale complexion. I said so, to which Aunt Bae responded with a chuckle, assuring me that was perfectly normal and that the full richness of her color would develop in no time at all. Although I have seldom seen a newborn resemble anything beyond a piece of precious putty, Bobbi Kristina did, even at that time, appear to favor her father for facial features. There was no doubt there.

The birthing process complete and the patient sewn up, it was time to convey the two back to the ward, a journey that would be the baby's first exposure to the public. As we proceeded through the hospital corridors with Whitney covered, and Bobbi Kristina totally concealed, it did not take long before some bright spark realized who was on the gurney and attempted to snap a photo. The result was merely a very shaky and blurred picture that may or may not have been a Black woman in a hospital bed, surrounded by suited men. The rest and substance of the story in the supermarket rag was mere speculation, supplemented by fervent imaginations and the usual barrel full of lies.

Safely back in her room, visitations by family and close friends began, and within a few days, to the utter horror and dismay of all, a perfect photograph of the baby in her bed in Whitney's room graced the front page of yet another tabloid. Absolutely impossible! This was not an off-chance snap by an outsider. This was someone on the inside, operating to Whitney's *and* the baby's detriment, and in favor of their own financial gain. To my mind, there could not have been a lower form of life in existence.

The nursing staff was grilled. Naturally, they did not carry pocket cameras with them as part of their official accoutrements, and cell phone cameras were still years away. John Houston was livid. I was not too happy either, as head of security, at this flagrant breach of privacy. As a licensed private investigator, I have many associates and contacts across the world. One happened to be an investigator who worked for the paper that published the photograph. Through him I learned that a check for $10,000 had been paid to the photographer. He told me that the endorsing signature on the back appeared to read "Pat Watson."

Pat was Gary's girlfriend at the time, and both had visited Whitney in her private room after the birth. Donna Houston confronted Pat, who denied having anything to do with the photograph, stating that she did not even own a camera. The matter was not pursued at corporate level and considered closed, but there was a general consensus as to who was actually to blame, and an understanding that Pat had simply been used as a pawn for the benefit of those with fewer scruples.

Cissy Houston would hear no wrong uttered against any of her children, so the obvious theory went unspoken and unaddressed for fear of incurring her wrath. The situation reinforced my belief that Whitney had more to fear from the enemy within than from those outside her inner circle. Ironically, Pat eventually married Gary and is now the executive who manages the estate, which continues to exploit Whitney to this day.

10

The Show Must Go On

When Bobbi Kristina was a mere three months old, we began two years of nonstop frenetic activity that made the previous touring regime seem like a walk in the park. Expanded world travel, concerts, meetings, interviews, special one-off appearances and events, a new batch of crazed fanatics, staff additions, challenges and changes, dramas, melodramas, near catastrophes, in-house bickering, and jockeying for position all combined to totally immerse the organization in an unprecedented level of intense activity and commitment. Even without the complexities associated with adding a new high-profile baby target to the fold, it would have been an improbable challenge. In retrospect, it is a wonder beyond belief that we ever passed through and prevailed. Perhaps *prevailed* is not the right word, as the grueling nature of that tour was one factor that led to Whitney's eventual inability to perform.

Robyn was replaced as Whitney's executive assistant by Laurie Badami, Aunt Bae's daughter. Laurie had recently lost both her husband and her job as a flight attendant for Delta Airlines. When she came on with us, she had not yet gained custody of her daughter. On first impression, I found her very amiable, capable, and professional.

She seemed to possess enough trepidation toward her new role that her intent and focus were purposeful, if not precisely through actual experience in the discipline. She was not afraid to ask for help. And she did.

The replacement of Robyn brought joy and celebration across the board. Relegated to producing tour jackets, she came up with something that looked like what a car mechanic might wear. The design was so dreadful—heavy faded blue canvas with a padded interior and graffiti-style writing on the back—that no one would wear it in public. She was left to flounder and would ultimately part ways with the organization and Whitney some years later.

Shelly Long, another of Aunt Bae's daughters, became Bobbi Kristina's nanny. She was a sweetheart, totally dedicated to the care of the baby and both highly tolerant and forgiving of the shortcomings and failures of those around her. Shelly had seen it all, been there, done that, and bought the T-shirt. Down to earth, she possessed some of her mother's finer qualities.

With the nanny came a female security officer named ROBERTA QUICK. A martial arts expert to some degree, she was recommended by Bobby Brown. Her interesting background included previously stabbing a former boyfriend in the neck, presumably with good cause, but something that perhaps should have prevented her from being hired in the first place. As with all employees, I was not briefed on them in advance, nor did I have the option of vetting before they simply appeared, fully signed up and raring to go, generally without the slightest idea of what their role really entailed. When I did identify something in an employee's history that could reflect poorly on Whitney, senior management typically paid no attention. Consequently, we were left to work with the ever-so-slightly defective tools with which we had been blessed.

One actual blessing in disguise came in the form of a replacement for my departed security assistant Smitty. I met the new guy on a day when the executive party members were all relaxing at Newport Beach Resort in Sunny Isles, Florida. The beach was packed with vacationers, and Whitney and her husband were out frolicking on Jet Skis in the bay, nicely out of reach of most, while I kept a peripheral distance on my Jet Ski to either intercept anyone getting too close or come to their rescue should one of the crafts malfunction or overturn. The couple were thoroughly enjoying themselves, and making a lot of noise so that everyone on the beach would know it was them out there, as was always the case with Bobby.

We returned to the shore, and I'd taken a seat in the sand with our group when I noticed a shadow looming over me. I turned and watched the approach of arguably the largest man I had ever seen. Robert Fontenot Jr. was the name of this veritable mountain of a man who, by a mere glare and knitting together of the eyebrows, could instill fear in any who laid eyes on him. I was grateful he was on my side and not a fan determined to get an autograph. I would have had my work cut out for me trying to stop him. This soft-spoken giant introduced himself as "Big Bob." As we talked, an exuberant beach vacationer recognized Whitney and thought it an opportune moment to approach her where she lay. Big Bob, seeing the man out of the corner of his eye, stared, scowled, and stuck out his arm, which was about the same size as my leg, but more muscular. The would-be interloper froze, turned, and walked away.

Hailing from Compton, near L.A., Big Bob was significantly different than the other newcomers. Despite his origins in what was reportedly a crime- and drug-infested hellhole, he was as clean as a whistle, as reliable and trustworthy as they come. His own man. A good man. He was a criminal justice major with a deep-seated sense of loyalty and professional application toward security, all supplemented by a great sense of humor. Over the years we worked together, his distracting and menacing mass proved extremely beneficial to us. Whitney and I could walk behind him and not be seen by anyone from the front.

By the time we had approached a crowd, not only did they naturally part at his approach, but he also totally captured the crowd's attention, holding them momentarily mesmerized, and we passed by them before they ever realized Whitney had been behind him.

———————

Whitney's commitments ramped up out of all reasonable proportion following the release of *The Bodyguard*. Her recording, touring, merchandising, fan club, charities, and promotional appearances were exceedingly demanding. The more one sat back and watched what was happening, in those rare moments one had the luxury to do so, the more apparent it became that Whitney was losing her identity as a young independent woman and mother. She was evolving more and more into a moneymaking machine at the behest of Clive Davis's Arista Records empire along with associated promoters and music industry executives. That delicate and unique voice box, and the beautiful frame in which it was housed, was a product being exploited, more and more mercilessly, in pursuit of the almighty dollar. It was almost as if the music business moguls had assessed a shelf life for her, and as such she was g oing to be fast-tracked to achieve and meet their self-serving goals, no matter what.

Being involved in my own business, I could understand the objectives. Once this talent had broken beyond repair, or lost earning capacity, they would have another one waiting to replace and exploit. But knowing Whitney's personality, I found the process more than a little sad and realized this was yet another element from which I was the least equipped to protect her. Would Whitney prevail? I so wished that for her, but even in 1993 the writing was on the wall and becoming clearer with each passing and escalating event.

———————

We slammed into action in early June, attending the MTV Movie Awards in Los Angeles, hosted by none other than Eddie Murphy. These types of events can be interesting as the stars tend to expound on their opinions and exemplify their privileged bias on one topic or another. For me, it was fun to watch those who felt they were better than, rather than simply different from, the rest of normal society. I recall Sharon Stone stumbling down the stairs at such an event and marveled at the number of lines in the face of Rod Stewart (but not as many as those so deeply and extensively etched in the countenance of Julio Iglesias, whom we had met in Paris).

From there we headed to the Renaissance Hotel in Washington, DC. In 1993 a new president was installed in the most powerful and influential chair in the world. William Jefferson Clinton chose Whitney, among others, to perform at a June presidential gala for the Democratic National Committee at the Washington Convention Center. Rehearsals commenced on Sunday, June 27, with Kenny G (a logical pick for the sax-playing president), Little Texas, and the Trumpeters.

On Tuesday, the event took place with all due pomp and ceremony. It was a treat for me and extremely interesting to work with the Secret Service and presidential security teams. We met with and shook the hands of the president and his wife, First Lady Hillary Clinton, and Vice President Gore and his wife, Tipper. From what I recall, Mr. Gore was wearing a rather ill-fitting suit on which he had fastened all the jacket buttons, and the trouser legs looked too short, making him appear uncomfortable. President Clinton was a sharp dresser and smooth talker, with a soft southern drawl and penetrating eyes. He greeted us all but paid special attention to Whitney, understandably. The show kicked off with Little Texas followed by Kenny G, with Mr. Clinton getting up onstage and doing a little bit of his own saxophone solo, and finally, Whitney. She finished out her set with a rendition of "Battle Hymn of the Republic," which I would not hesitate in deeming the best version I'd ever heard. Judging from the applause and the energy in the room, everyone there thought so as well. Then came boring speeches, and we went back to the hotel with a flight to New Jersey in the morning to prepare for whatever came next.

———————

Laurie was rapidly becoming familiar with her role of inducing Whitney to acquiesce to the will of others, which at Nippy Inc. was one of the responsibilities of the executive assistant. But the stress of the task lay heavily on her. Laurie was less argumentative than Robyn was, and being an empathetic person by nature, she took conflict personally. This was an endearing quality, but she often lacked the diplomacy to achieve the desired result, especially when Whitney and her husband wanted to do things one way and senior management wanted something different. Laurie found solace, friendship, and ultimately what she perceived to be love with Tommy Wattley, Whitney's longtime and dedicated chauffeur. Their relationship was perhaps an error in judgment on both their parts, as it was then apparent that Laurie was being pulled in one direction by her duties as Whitney's assistant when she would prefer to go in another with Tommy.

Once intimacy became a factor, so did jealousy and domestic disputes with Tommy, who had a reputation as a player. This, in accordance with the well-founded advice about not dumping on one's own doorstep, only made Laurie's job more difficult. So the rest of us often ended up having to deal with two domestic disputes—Whitney and Bobby's, and Laurie and Tommy's—at the same bloody time. Laurie's initial work ethic went out the window the minute she jumped into bed with Tommy, and the high hopes I'd originally had for her were dashed. The relationship also seemed to cause Laurie to increase her use of Mary Jane and other mother's little helpers. Aunt Bae was Laurie's saving grace, as she did everything in her power to retain Whitney's faith and confidence in her daughter's abilities. On top of looking after the baby with her other daughter, Aunt Bae was placed under considerable additional stress.

All these issues were precursors to a crescendo of disaster.

———————

The first section of the tour kicked off with a show in Miami. The entire group was housed at the Freeport Hotel and sweating through the days and nights, with high humidity in the Florida summer being the norm, exacerbated daily by the obligatory thirty-minute 4:00 PM torrential downpour and immediate drying to add more moisture to the overwhelming mess of the tropical environment. The show was a veritable disaster in that Whitney had insisted on no air-conditioning in the auditorium. Tour manager Tony Bulluck—after some intense discussions with the venue personnel—forced them to acquiesce to a request that was selfish, unreasonable, and absolutely out of order in such a tropical environment, despite Whitney's insistence that the reason was to protect her voice box. The result was a rather shameful booing by the audience due to their unified sweaty discomfort.

Whitney received negative publicity the day after the concert, but she remained unapologetic. From her perspective, she was starting a grueling tour schedule that would again cover many climates, and she felt obligated to protect her voice above all other concerns. At least, that was the official explanation. Luckily, there was no one she could not win over with her rendition of "I Will Always Love You," even if people had to sit in puddles of their own sweat to enjoy it.

Looking back, perhaps it is a shame that her concern for her vocal cords was not a greater consideration in determining what to do (and what *not* to do) to avoid injuring the delicate moneymaking organ upon which so many relied.

———————

From Miami we headed to Virginia, Boston, and then to five shows at Radio City Music Hall in New York City. One evening in New York, we were traveling to our hotel in a convoy of two vehicles, with Whitney and her husband in the lead, security being pressed to travel in the second vehicle through some temperamental quirk that had developed during the evening. En route, our small convoy was rapidly overtaken by a yellow cab, forcing the lead Range Rover to decelerate and come to a halt to avoid an inevitable impact. The backup vehicle likewise immediately stopped, but left enough space for the Range Rover to back out and leave if need be. Four scruffily dressed males leaped from the cab and started to approach Whitney's vehicle. I was out of the car in a heartbeat and moving to intercept the menacing men. This did not look good at all.

Although not authorized to carry a concealed firearm in New York State, I nevertheless did. I felt it essential for the protection of my principal, and by now being fully assured of the power and effect of Whitney's array of attorneys, I was certain they would be able to establish justification for possession and necessary use if the need should arise. Surely, no matter how stupid people can be, autograph hunters would not be likely to steal a taxicab to pursue and stop a high-profile personality's vehicle. They clearly had more sinister intentions. I started to reach for my Sig Sauer .380, hidden in a pancake holster on my right hip. I prepared for a confrontation with this bunch of idiots, intending to meet force with like force. I had my hand inside my jacket when they all started shouting, "Police! Police!"

I was not sure whether they were calling for the police against my approach or seeking to pose as actual police officers themselves. At that juncture the lead male produced, from a chain around his neck, what appeared to be a badge and credentials, followed immediately by a similar action by his three colleagues, all of whom had slowed at the ferocity of my approach. Now all were repeatedly shouting "Police!" and gesturing to signal a "stop and relax" demand. They held a crouched and legs-apart stance, as did I. I stood in front of Whitney's Range Rover, between what I perceived as the threat and her. We were in a standoff situation, everyone with one hand in the air, the other on whatever was underneath our jackets.

I knew chauffeur Tommy was fully aware of the protocol I demanded and that he was expected to reverse, removing Whitney from the danger, which I would engage with to facilitate her safe escape. Seeing the police badges, he did not leave but rather waited to see what would happen. We stood there for a few seconds. I waited, ready. At this point the lead officer spoke, admitting a mistaken identity event. I still wasn't convinced but heard him out. Apparently they were looking for a similar vehicle that had reportedly recently engaged in a drug-related transaction in the vicinity. We all finally relaxed.

They were an undercover squad, hence the taxi. I was relieved that they didn't inquire as to what exactly I was reaching for inside my jacket, and the encounter certainly reinforced my sense of just how quickly things could go tits-up. In the aftermath of the event, I reflected on how "bad" their information was. I was aware that the Range Rover with Tommy, Bobby Brown, and others had been parked and minimally active on the streets of the city for quite a few hours that evening. Had something taken place that gave the police cause to suspect and react the way they had? By this stage in the game, nothing would have surprised me. As we had avoided a serious situation by the skin of our teeth, I chose not to make a report and put this one on the back burner for the time being. If anything similar happened in the future, I'd have this incident to include in my report and bolster my interpretation of events.

The tour limped and bounced its way along, and we found ourselves showing at the Meadowlands in New Jersey, Whitney's home turf.

This was an important affair for the Houstons, and all family members duly turned up as Whitney was getting ready to perform. The dressing room soon became crowded as they stayed longer than necessary before leaving to take their allotted VIP seats. I was mildly surprised that John Houston had decided to bring his new wife to this show, breaking the family's pact that John would not have her at events Cissy would be attending.

The young wife's unprecedented arrival that evening was precisely the moment when things started to turn sour. I had assumed that the original agreement between the warring former spouses had been relaxed, but I couldn't have been more wrong. Cissy became dark and explosive in mood, uttering her complaints loud enough for everyone to hear. It was not what Whitney wanted to see, hear, or become involved with before going onstage.

Cissy, however, did not take her daughter's needs into consideration on this occasion. She was nothing remotely akin to reasonable when things did not go her way. The young wife was escorted to her seat, a considerable distance from Cissy's. The tension backstage was palpable. Cissy clearly was on a mission, and we all secretly feared how it might manifest. The show started and Whitney was doing her thing. Despite any inner turmoil or strife created by her mother, she was, as always, perfection.

I often used to think that when Whitney was onstage and singing, she escaped from her offstage reality and entered her own world where she could live and perform with her heart. There were more than a few occasions that a serious preshow drama, familial or otherwise, had threatened to destroy an event, but once she took to the stage, no performance was ever adversely affected by what had taken place even moments earlier. Onstage, Whitney was at home, in her skin, where she belonged and where she loved to be.

As the performance progressed, I received a message requesting urgent assistance in the car park. This type of call was extremely unusual. When Whitney performed, I never left my spot in the wings. She always knew where to find me and often checked to make sure I was there. I took a quick look in front of the stage and, lo and behold, Cissy was not in her seat.

I arrived at the VIP parking compound to find Cissy Houston smashing John's two-door Jaguar with her walking stick. She had already destroyed the windshield, mirrors, and headlights. The body-work was starting to look as if it had been used in a demolition derby. As she maneuvered around the destroyed vehicle, slamming it repeatedly with the stick, she was screaming about John's "shoeless bitch maid money-grabbing whore" and how John should never have brought her to the show, any show, anytime, anywhere.

The scene was unbelievable and, for a split second, left me completely stunned. I approached very tentatively, believing that in her current state of mind she would have no hesitation in identifying me as yet another conspiratorial ally of John and use the damned cane on me. From a safe distance I raised my voice and implored her to stop. She saw me and continued beating the vehicle while looking directly at me, a focused fury beaming from her eyes. As she turned to inflict another blow, I caught the stick from behind as it was raised over her shoulder and, by simply preventing the flow of her actions, she lost her rhythm and likewise her strength. Thank heavens!

I took her arm and escorted her back into the building, where Michael came to take charge of his mother. John seemed unmoved by what Cissy had done to his car. Anyone else might have called the police and had her charged. John, however, stoically and resignedly did not do so. Perhaps he was grateful that his ex-wife had not physically directed her hatred and malice, woefully underestimated by him, at his new wife or, indeed, at him.

Suffice it to say, I don't recall seeing the wife at another show, or anywhere else with John for that matter. Whitney was terribly upset, and Michael was beside himself. Aunt Bae was in tears as she saw the beloved family in such a dysfunctional state. The entire crew was out of sorts, and the evening was not soon forgotten. We left in darkness, by coach, and moved on overnight to the next show. That was the way we did things.

The never-ending tour continued. We spent the first half of August in Europe, then returned to the States for two weeks of shows in California. On August 29 we were off to Osaka, Japan. Three continents in one timeline-crisscrossing month. A ferocious itinerary.

As we waited in the VIP lounge at JFK airport to board the plane to Japan, Whitney's hairdresser, Carol Ensminger, approached me. She was looking more worried than usual in anticipation of the flights. A reformed heroin addict and former prostitute, Carol had a tough life but had beaten the odds and was one of the sweetest and most down-to-earth people ever to tour with us. I so enjoyed her company. Straight-talking, honest, streetwise, and funny, everyone loved Carol, and she was especially close to Aunt Bae.

The funniest thing about Carol was her reaction to a fire alarm going off in any one of our hotels, and they often did. Having a serious phobia of fires, she would fly out of her room as if fired from a circus cannon. Carrying nothing but her passport, she would hightail it out of there with strides that would humble an Olympian, even though it was a false alarm every single time. And we all cracked up every single time.

At the airport, Carol asked to speak with me privately. She was clearly anxious about something. I wondered whether her flight phobia (yes, she suffered from that as well) was manifesting into a need for some kind words and assurances before boarding. She looked at me and told me that she had been called on to conceal a stash of narcotics inside her vagina for the trip to Japan, to be used while there.

I was mortified. At the same time, I realized that this was probably something that had happened on previous trips. Not one customs officer had ever stopped and searched any of the ladies of Whitney's executive party. However, in Japan's Tokyo-Narita Airport, Whitney's chauffeur Tommy had been searched once on entry. The remains of a mainly smoked roach were discovered in the folds of his briefcase's inner lining, an oversight by Tommy and not an attempt to smuggle narcotics into the country. However, it was certainly considered serious by the Japanese authorities, and Tommy was handcuffed at the counter and marched off by six Japanese police officers, the lead one holding the offending roach above his head, barely visible between his pinched thumb and forefinger. A couple of hours and attorneys later, along with a whole load of fussing by Whitney's assistant Laurie Badami, Tommy was released without charge. Such is the power of the Nippy legal machine in action.

It was that event, and the fact that we were returning to the same Japanese airport, that worried Carol the most. She was petrified, and her natural paranoia convinced her she would be the one charged with international drug smuggling on this occasion. I asked her for whom she was carrying the narcotics. She said it was a member of the executive party, claiming the request came directly from Whitney. I told Carol that she should say nothing to anyone and remove and dispose of the products by flushing them down the toilet before boarding. She could explain later that they had fallen out when she used the bathroom on the plane. I was not sure whether such a manner of loss could possibly be a reasonable excuse, but Carol seemed grateful and went to the lounge bathroom.

No more was ever said about the incident, but for me, there was never another plane journey when I did not think about it and wonder. I had given countless security warning briefs to the tour members regarding the dire consequences of transporting narcotics anywhere, especially into other countries. I had quoted the law in Singapore, where drug smugglers could be executed. So they all knew the risks. Yet through Carol, I learned that drugs had been and would continue to be transported across international boundaries, and to my horror had been so inserted—literally—into Singapore during our tour there. So rather than anticipating a visit from the famous Uncle Weeder, as in the early days, it appeared that strategy had evolved to ensure said uncle was a permanent tour member traveling with us "undercover."

———————

Bobby and Whitney would often endure stints of separation, reportedly for professional reasons pertaining to their individual careers— although the more time passed, the more Bobby's career dwindled while Whitney's rose to new heights. On September 6, 1993, Whitney was preparing for her first show in Tokyo after a double in Osaka. Bobbi Kristina was not yet six months old. Whitney was thrilled when Bobby, accompanied by his assistant James, arrived at the Capitol Hotel Tokyu, and the day had been a good one.

After but a few hours, as we were all getting ready for the show, I saw James bustling down the corridor looking demented and on a mission. It appeared that after a flight from hell and a couple of hours in bed, Bobby had announced that he had to return to the United States immediately for "business purposes." Unbelievable! Traveling all that way just to get his rocks off, and then a return journey for something that sounded highly questionable. Whitney went ballistic. We were all ready to leave for the show when this "important business trip" announcement was made and things began to grind to a painful, angry halt.

Whitney's assistant Silvia and the other ladies were consoling Whitney, who had longed to see her husband, and probably paid for the first-class tickets, only to be so badly used and then threatened with abandonment in what, at best, was a mean-spirited move by Bobby. If business was so pressing for him, why the hell had he flown out anyway? In all the shouting and screaming, and as the minutes ticked down toward showtime, we had a major problem developing: Whitney seemed to have little intention of going onstage. I went to the suite door where Silvia stood, looking worried.

Damn it—I lost it. I shouted through the door, "We are supposed to be professionals! Has no one ever heard that for professionals the show must go on?"

It went very quiet on the inside.

I stormed away, wondering how the hell I was going to explain this to John Houston and the executives back in New Jersey, or to our Japanese promoters, and hating Bobby with a vengeance for what he was doing not only to his wife personally and professionally but also to those involved in promoting her career and reputation. While attempting to contain my anger, I was explaining the situation to our staff and drivers when Whitney burst out of the room. "The show must go on. Let's go, people!"

She had clearly been crying, but damn, she was angry. Fuming, in fact, and she held Bobbi Kristina close to her as we marched through the hotel and out to the vehicles, our drivers now scrambling to retain their readiness. I was aware that Bobby was following, sulking, with a face that looked like a smacked arse. Apparently his urgent "business meeting" was no longer so urgent. He was staying, and all James could do when I looked at him was shrug his shoulders.

That night, the fans were treated to Whitney taking the baby onstage and singing one of her love songs to little Bobbi Kristina— one that she normally sang to her husband, calling him onstage. But that night she pointedly ignored him, and he got the message. He stood in the wings looking sheepish. It was one of the few times I saw Whitney dig in her heels against his misogynistic, selfish ways.

———————

Whitney performed some forty-two concerts between July 5 and September 22. We had traveled for 261 days on the tour and still had 104 more scheduled for this leg alone. Whitney continued to demand no air-conditioning at many of her venues. The two-hour shows, with short wardrobe changes and approximately twenty to thirty minutes of gospel music, required so much from Whitney. The pitch, volume, and sustained pressure of the notes were so feverish and passionate, it made me cringe when I thought of the stress this part of the performance put on her voice box.

She frequently came off the stage with sweat coming from her pores as if someone had turned a faucet on her head, covered in towels that were quickly drenched, and unable to speak a single word. Being hoarse is barely an adequate description of her after-show state; she was physically and emotionally drained, yet aware that in a few hours she would need to do the same routine all over again. And she seldom missed a note in those days. You had to be there to appreciate it, as indeed hundreds of thousands were over the early years. I have heard many recount their experiences at her shows with total wonderment. Whitney was a truly special lady, and when she was in the gospel moment, there was nothing and no one that could stop her.

11

Soaring and Sinking

As I look back on the second half of the Bodyguard World Tour, I see now how Whitney's precipitous rise was simultaneously the making of her eventual fall. She had reached heights of fame unimaginable, won a roomful of awards, made millions upon millions, and was known and loved the world over. Added to that were other factors: the man she chose to marry, the people she surrounded herself with, the insidious nature of the greed sudden wealth breeds, the stresses of new motherhood, and the pressure to consistently perform beyond her physical capability. These combined to create a perfect storm for Whitney. The next few months were a ping-pong game of ups and downs, public triumphs, and private tribulations. From the outside, Whitney looked to be on top of the world. But something very different was happening on the inside.

From Japan we traveled to Bangkok, then Singapore, to complete the Far East portion of the tour. After a short break we headed to London for the European leg. Between October 5 and November 29, we played in England, Ireland, Belgium, Spain, Switzerland, Germany, Norway, Holland, Austria, and France, this time traveling by private jet rather than commercial flights. I was quite pleased because this is the safest way of moving one's principal about, airports being one of the least controllable environments. We remained far from crowds and paparazzi, with a limousine straight from the plane to the hotel, passports handled solely by me, and an ability to easily alter flight plans to suit our needs. We defeated any attempt by the media to obtain prior knowledge of our routes. It was a CP officer's dream come true. At last, we were getting serious about this stuff.

At the Frankfurt Hotel in Germany, I decided to take a break and have a beer at the bar, a treat I seldom allowed myself. I was sitting there waiting to meet with our drivers to discuss plans for show and travel movements when Bobby Brown came in and sat next to me, wearing what to me appeared to be a colorful, skull-tight tea cozy on his head. *Strange*, I thought.

"Hey, David. I've seen a light. I'm being guided in a good direction." He then told me he was changing all his ways accordingly. He had found new meaning to life through a sudden belief in Allah, and he was henceforth going to practice the lifestyle and religious pursuits of a Muslim. I was somewhat taken aback and more than a little skeptical. Yet there he was, suitably attired and with no drink in his hand, in a bar, and proclaiming for himself what I believed to be the most punitive alternative lifestyle in comparison to the one he had indulged in up to that point.

I congratulated him and wished him well, and he was off, seemingly very happy and at peace with himself. Some three hours later, I was walking through the hotel doing my rounds, when here he came with two women, one on each arm, clearly working girls. Inwardly, I had to smile to myself. Not quite what Allah had in mind, perhaps, for his most recent convert.

To my surprise, he offered me one of the girls. I thanked him and declined, and off he went, leaving me to ponder how this latest scenario was going to play out. Sure enough, a few minutes later, here comes James, Bobby's assistant, having been thrown out of his room for Bobby to use temporarily as he looked after his girls. Of course, James could hardly take Bobby's place in Whitney's room, so he remained in the hotel lounge. I went to bed. So much for the "changing of the ways" and the new Muslim lifestyle.

Although I found some humor in this antic of Bobby's, over time, his acting out only increased, and wore us all down. Whitney, of course, was the most affected by him, but by the same token, she was the one who loved him, who kept him there with us. And it seemed that the worse it got with Bobby, the more she dug in with her determination not to give up. In retrospect, I can see that his ever-so-brief foray into Islam was part of his search for something to call his own. Bobby's career was going nowhere, in complete contrast to Whitney's. He lived unhappily in her shadow. He was insecure and lost, looking, but never finding anything good. On the contrary, he looked to his vices for relief, dragging Whitney down with him.

We returned to the States for the Billboard Music Awards in L.A., where Whitney broke that event's record, winning eleven awards, including #1 World Artist. She showed the audience exactly why she deserved all of them with her rendition of "I Have Nothing," which she belted out in a breathtaking crescendo, bringing the entire auditorium to a standing ovation well before she'd finished the song. From there, she strode to the podium, perspiration glistening across her face, to receive her final award. Someone handed her the wrong sheet of paper, so she had to wing it with her thank-yous, which she did with her signature grace and endearing style.

After a brief break for the holidays, we started off 1994 with our first visit to South America, beginning in São Paulo, Brazil, a place of extreme criminal notoriety. At night we could hear gunshots ringing out in the large park immediately behind the hotel. The show was held at an outdoor arena on January 16. Whitney was singing when some idiot fan emerged from the curtains and ran straight onto the stage toward her. I was there in seconds, grabbed him around the neck, and dragged him off the stage, bouncing him down the stairs as roughly as I could manage without losing balance. Employing a "come-with-me" wristlock from the old police days in London, I escorted him, dancing on his toes, to the exit through stunned crew members. At the main entrance, after a final tweak and tear or snap of the wrist, I hurtled him into the crowd outside the gate, never to be seen again.

It was later determined that he had been a local crew member who had climbed the stage scaffolding internally, behind the struc-ture screening, in order to dart out onto the stage. I did apologize in advance to Sheldon Platt for any legal issues that could have arisen, in that I may have broken the guy's wrist. The attorney was singularly unconcerned with that, but all were deeply troubled with the breach in stage security protocols. Latin America was an entirely different kettle of fish. The fans were passionate in a way unique to Latin culture, and the lax attitude toward security made incompetence appear like a badge of honor being worn by many.

The very next day, January 17, 1994, California experienced a 6.7 magnitude earthquake, causing serious structural damage. The epicen-ter was in the San Fernando Valley of Los Angeles County, where many members of the band and crew lived. Our guitarist, Carlos, later told us that his house's chimney stack was knocked through the roof, landing directly across the entire length of his bed. Had he been in bed at the time, he most likely would not have survived. Other staff members were likewise affected, causing a somewhat somber mood as we packed up and moved on to Rio.

I found that the old and worn-out infrastructure of Rio de Janeiro no longer did justice to the city's reputation. Furthermore, it was just as lawless as São Paulo. From our hotel, we had a direct view of both the beach made famous by so many renditions of "Copacabana" and the barrio villages on the surrounding hills. One would think the contrast between the poorest shantytowns and the world-renowned beach would be acute, but it was not when you saw the dilapidated streets, broken walkways, and the equally broken people walking along the water's edge. An altogether squalid-looking place, and not at all what I had imagined when I'd hummed "Girl from Ipanema."

One morning, I accompanied Whitney and Bobby to the Atlantis Restaurant on a terrace in front of the swimming pool at the Rio Palace Hotel in Copacabana. As we entered, I noticed a face I recognized. Ronald Biggs had planned and carried out what came to be known as the Great Train Robbery of 1963. He and his gang successfully robbed a London train carrying mail and walked away with some £2.6 million. He was subsequently apprehended and held at Wandsworth Prison in London, until he escaped in 1964 by climbing the wall with a rope ladder. He made it to Brazil, which did not have an extradition agreement with the UK at the time, and had been living there ever since. He was a showman, considering himself a personality and a local hero, a wanted man who could walk about as free as the wind.

Sitting at a table with a group of people and conversing about his recently published memoir *Odd Man Out* was none other than the villain himself. Big-framed, tanned, and sporting a thin gray ponytail, he was dressed in a yellow short-sleeved shirt and white pants. His face was lumpy with age, his large bulbous nose pitted and drink-ravaged. Out of the corner of my eye, I observed him identify Whitney and Bobby as he imitated a camera's operating action, silently mouthing to one of his companions that he wanted to have his photograph taken with them. I quickly told Whitney and Bobby who he was as he made his approach. Whitney was amused and Bobby thought it was great fun, urging me to "arrest him." This thought actually crossed my mind with some hilarity. If only it were possible, what an outcome that would be for Mr. Slipper back home. Jack Slipper, former head of the Robbery Squad of the Metropolitan Police, was the officer in charge of the Great Train Robbery investigation. His lifelong ambition to recapture the escapee Biggs is now a matter of British police history.

As he neared our table, I rose and deliberately stood in his way, preventing his progress. He leaned against me and poked his head around my left shoulder, introducing himself to Whitney as the Great Train Robber. In her usual fabulously casual manner, Whitney was courteous, acknowledging his forced introduction with a smile. "Yes. I know," she replied in a polite but clearly dismissive manner. His time was already up.

As he turned to leave, I took my opportunity. His ear being no more than three inches from my mouth, I said in a low voice, "Let me introduce myself to you, Mr. Biggs. I am Sergeant Roberts from the Special Patrol Group of the Metropolitan Police at New Scotland Yard. Mr. Slipper sends his best regards and asks how it feels to know that everywhere you go, you are being watched." He froze.

Granted, I'd indulged in a bit of a white lie in that I should have used the word *former* before the word *sergeant*, but what the hell, Biggs was no stranger to falsehood and prevarication. His big old ugly face turned red with rage. His minder grabbed him and dragged him from the table and away from the event. Whitney, Bobby, and I all had a good laugh over it. These moments of laughter were what carried us through. The never-ending and grueling nature of that tour demanded levity from time to time, and I tried to provide it where I could.

———

The first leg of the South American tour over, it was back to the United States to prepare for a host of upcoming events. It began with the February birthday party for Bobby Brown, held at the famous Tavern on the Green in New York's Central Park. It was clear that Whitney was trying to flatter Bobby's sense of pride by throwing him this party, squeezed in between the two legs of our South American tour and right in the middle of awards season, which she absolutely dominated that year. As I look back and reflect, I can see that it was precisely this endearing part of Whitney's nature, her need to give, to make sure the people around her were taken care of, that ended up harming her. Rather than show appreciation, rather than give back, so many only took advantage.

With a guest list of more than five hundred, matters were complicated by the fact that the Tavern would not exclusively be ours. There were expected to be a hundred guests not associated with the event in other parts of the establishment. Our guest list included Thicknezz, Shorti 1 Forti, Big Ange, El Boog-E, Wreckx-n-Effect, Boyz II Men, Bell Biv DeVoe, DJ Jazzy Jeff, Jellybean, Naughty by Nature, Whodini, Full Force, Jodeci, Jack the Rapper, Patra, Heavy D, Run-DMC, Salt-N-Pepa, Mary J. Blige, and Kool G Rap in the hip-hop category, along with Harry Belafonte, Anita Baker, Quincy Jones, Spike Lee, L.A. Reid & Babyface, Debbie Winans, and the like. The evening promised to be very interesting. Much reliance was to be placed on Garelick Security working in tandem with the local NYPD to control what was expected to be a raucous affair, commencing at 9:00 PM and scheduled to continue through 3:00 the following morning. Against better advice, the baby was also going to attend.

On the night in question, the guests began to arrive, dressed in various colorful and flamboyant outfits, many appearing to want to upstage their peers. Quite a few wore oversized T-shirts and jeans with the crotches at the level of the knees, making attempts to walk difficult and somewhat comical. The value of such sizing, especially if trying to run, was completely lost on me. As the evening wore on, guests stumbled around holding bottles of Dom Pérignon champagne by the neck, as one might hold a bottle of beer at a weekend barbecue. The music was so damned loud that it made me wonder how on earth people could have a conversation without screaming at each other. I was somewhat concerned about the effect on the baby, too.

Bobby and Whitney held hands, carrying the baby between them, as they did their meet-and-greet rounds with the guests, with Bobby being the center of attention and Whitney sometimes looking out of place. There were some strange smells—aromatic and herbal—permeating the environment from time to time, together with questionable attendance by any number of persons in the same toilet cubicle, all of whom exited as if suffering from a cold, sniffing and snorting their way out of the bathroom. The security screening to enter the festivities prioritized weapons over illegal substances. In the end, a good time was had, and the event passed without much trouble. We stayed overnight in New York City and left the next day for Mendham, back to the work of making money to pay for such excessive extravagances, as was Whitney's wont.

February and March of 1994 were dominated by awards ceremonies where Whitney received a heavy, and in some cases unprecedented, showering of recognition. At the American Music Awards, she surprised the audience by lending her deep and golden voice to Gershwin's "I Loves You, Porgy." She then went on to win seven of the eight awards she was up for, accepting them humbly and happily, once with Bobbi Kristina on her hip. Her final award that night was the Merit Award, and she didn't quite succeed in holding back tears when her good friend Stevie Wonder presented it to her. After thanking her God, as she always did, she added, "I sing because he blesses me," and she dedicated the award to her fans.

From there it was the Grammys, where she stood statuesque on a huge glass pedestal in a glittering white floor-length dress and blew us all away again, giving everything she had to the song that never failed to lift hearts and touch deep, "I Will Always Love You." And finally, on March 15, 1994, Whitney put it back in the faces of those who had booed her five years earlier at the Soul Train Music Awards. Upon receiving the Sammy Davis Jr. Entertainer of the Year Award, she strode to the podium and announced, "I have something to say." Her speech was eloquent and purposeful. She looked powerful, proud, and regal in a long body-hugging purple dress, with matching above-the-elbow gloves and a bejeweled head wrap. She had bided her time and stood up for herself at just the right moment, reminding the audience how Sammy Davis Jr. had endured racism as well as "insults aimed at him by his *own* people who blamed him for trying to rise above the ignorance and hatred, not with rhetoric but through his work." Just like Whitney herself did.

One thing that struck me about her speech that night was the very last thing she said before leaving the stage. "I thank my Heavenly Father for being better to me than I've been to myself." In retrospect it is clear that even at the pinnacle of her career, Whitney's self-awareness ran deep, her word choices both meaningful and tragically prescient.

In April we diverted to what was, for me, one of the most stunning one-off events we ever attended—and there were many. The 1994 Rainforest Foundation benefit at Carnegie Hall was organized by Sting and his wife, both of whom were renowned for their philanthropy. The show commenced with Sting himself, followed by Elton John, James Taylor, and Italian flutist Andrea Griminelli, who accompanied Taylor as he sang "Oh, What a Beautiful Mornin'." Then came the stunningly beautiful voice of Aaron Neville, followed by Tammy Wynette, Luciano Pavarotti, Larry Cox, Larry Adler, and Branford Marsalis. Whitney ended the show, accompanied by her full band, with a heartfelt delivery of "I Will Always Love You."

Playing her voice like the musical instrument it was, fingers flut-
tering as she let the spirit move her and improvising as the occasion demanded, she drew thunderous applause. But what was most
memorable for me came immediately prior when, spontaneously and
without rehearsing as far as I was aware, she joined Pavarotti onstage
for "Nessun dorma." Whitney contributed an incredible drawn-out
soprano, sounding as if she had studied opera. The look on Pavarotti's
face was one of utter astonishment at the perfection of Whitney's voice.
It almost made him falter, and certainly took everyone else's breath
away. I had heard her sing just about every genre of music there is,
but notwithstanding her unsurpassed passion and ability with gospel
music, this blew my mind. It almost seemed as if Whitney herself
was surprised. The performance demanded an ovation, led by the
man himself.

I had stood next to the vast-framed Pavarotti backstage as he waited
his turn to go on and was somewhat annoyed by the fussing he was
receiving at the hands of an assistant. Pavarotti was a man who sweated
profusely, and especially so under the heat of studio lighting. His
diminutive attendant was buzzing around him with a towel, trying
to mop his brow and wipe the sweat running freely from his face and
neck. Pavarotti himself was scowling at the man's incessant efforts,
swatting at him as one would an irritating fly. The poor assistant was
matching Pavarotti, sweat drop for sweat drop, and still he persisted
despite the protestations, rebukes, and scowls, accompanied by the-
atrical Italian gesturing.

The entire evening was a definitive life highlight for me. After the
show, we attended a party at the Central Park home of Sting and his
good lady, a vast and beautiful apartment encompassing two conjoined
units, one above the other. It was definitely a night to remember for
all fortunate enough to have been there, and a resounding success for
the charity. Remembering this incredible night in retrospect, I cannot
help but think of what Whitney could have been and done had the

stars not aligned to push her down. The star pushing the hardest was, perhaps, Whitney herself.

During some downtime at home in New Jersey between the two halves of the South American leg of the tour, I went to dinner with a girlfriend. In Brazil I had bought her a ring and set of earrings made of semiprecious stones. As we finished our meal, I took out the jewelry to give to her. She stood up quickly, knocking the table and spilling our bottle of champagne all over my trousers. She then started shouting, "I will, I will, I will!" to applause from our fellow diners.

I was concerned with being soaking wet and uncomfortable around the crotch and attempting to adjust myself accordingly to the point that the "I will" nonsense and associated clapping did not register with me immediately. I thought the restaurant's customers were applauding my discomfort. But then she threw her arms around my shoulders, and it became apparent that we were going to get married, as she had accepted my incorrectly interpreted, nonverbal proposal.

Holy crap! It was just costume jewelry, but there was no way for her to know that. In those dreadful few seconds, the die was cast and I was doomed, being far too chivalrous to balk and ruin the night for her. Absent some form of divine intervention, I submitted to the adage *such is life*. I was soon to be wed for a third time.

So a few months later, I decided to embark upon yet another cataclysmic error of life. I honored the spilled champagne commitment I had not verbally made. I felt obligated to follow through. I suppose overall, I was a glutton for punishment. Perhaps that was one thing Whitney and I had in common: choosing poorly and marrying for the wrong reasons. Originally scheduled for April Fool's Day, the event was moved to March 31. In a local town hall in Florham Park, after half a bottle of gin, I stupidly said "I do." Again.

I had not told Whitney of my intent to marry, and that was on purpose. I had come to note, with acute embarrassment and more than a little anger, how others in our touring family would purposefully await an opportunity to marry or celebrate an event while on the road, thereby effectively ensuring that Whitney would foot the bill. I thought this ploy manipulative and yet another example of people taking the opportunity to exploit her good-heartedness. I wanted nothing to do with that nonsense, so, like most other things in my life, I kept it private.

On Tuesday, April 12, Whitney and I were seated in the VIP lounge at JFK waiting to board a plane back to South America. We were talking, and I casually responded to her question as to what I had done over Easter. With my typical British humor, I said something to the effect of "Nothing much, boss. I just got married."

It was like I had slapped her hard across the face. I was shocked by her response. She looked as angry as I had ever seen her, almost speechless, and as if she were contemplating a way she could beat the crap out of me. As her eyes narrowed, I knew I had made a mistake and was in deep trouble. Finally, after a silence so heavy that even a pneumatic drill would not pierce it, she said, "Why didn't you tell me?!"

Again, with a sort of British flippancy attempting to lighten an extremely dark moment, I stupidly replied, "But I just did!"

Not a clever response at all. Now she said with menace, "Stop it. You know what I mean."

And so I acquiesced and told her the truth. I explained how I was upset by everyone using her kindness to their own personal advantage and to her detriment. Put simply, and on principle alone, I told her I found the practice abhorrent and wholly objectionable to my very being and I'd made a conscious decision not to tell her. I do not think she even knew I had girlfriends. She only knew that everything in my personal life was a distant second to my professional life—my protection of her and her child.

She listened quietly. She contemplated what I had said and, I believe, was putting a lot of thought into precisely what I meant. In her heart, I believe she knew, and if she didn't exactly agree, certainly understood an alternative perspective to that of her own. She softened and said, "Still, you should have told me."

She didn't qualify the statement as to why I should have done so, and I certainly did not ask. I simply said, "Yes, I should have perhaps. I'm sorry, boss."

Thankfully, at that precise juncture, our boarding was called and we were off to Santiago, Chile, for the second half of our South American tour. Whitney and I never again spoke of my getting married without telling her. But three months later, on arriving at the Four Seasons in Los Angeles, I was taken unawares by a surprise birthday party set up for me in one of the hotel rooms and attended by my wife.

Whitney had conspired with her and paid for the party without my knowledge. I think that was her way of telling me, *This is what I do for my people.* And it was. This lady was as gracious, humble, and caring as they come, notwithstanding her superstar status. She could equally present as a diva from hell, should the mood take her. It didn't happen too often, but for those who experienced it, such confrontational events were not easily forgotten.

———————

We showed in Santiago, Chile; Buenos Aires, Argentina; Caracas, Venezuela; and finished off in San Juan, Puerto Rico, where, on the night of April 24, we were lucky to escape with our lives. The performance was held at an outdoor arena, with local security staff who were as incompetent as they come. Rather than work, they were there to have fun. As the encore came to a conclusion, the crowd managed to breach the barriers and the masses moved as one toward the stage, screaming and shouting.

Local security personnel had been positioned to handle this possibility—all for naught. If they assisted us at all, it was purely by falling down and slowing the advancing fans slightly as they swarmed over them. It was probably the worst security we had encountered anywhere in the world at that time. There was utter pandemonium, and delay in thought or action by our team could have resulted in catastrophic consequences. With literally seconds to spare, we bundled Whitney into the limousine and we were off through the rear entrance, with the quickest of the wild fanatics managing to catch up and bang on the car with their hands and fists.

And with that, we wrapped up our South American tour.

In June and July we toured the United States, visiting New York, Connecticut, Ohio, Pennsylvania, Rhode Island, Michigan, Illinois, Georgia, Texas, Colorado, New Mexico, California, Washington, and Oregon. Whitney, the gel that kept the unwieldy tour machine together and rolling, was falling apart and losing traction emotionally and physically. As she anguished over her demons, the tour became blighted by show cancellations due to a host of issues, including illness, loss of voice, the ever-present husband-induced stress, problems with dryness of clime affecting her vocal cords, and even a reported pregnancy that turned out to be anything but. It was July in Texas, and Whitney believed she was pregnant and miscarrying. Her ob-gyn from Livingston, New Jersey, arrived at the hotel and examined her. He came out of her room and declared to a number of the executives gathered that she had never really been pregnant.

I wondered if this phantom pregnancy came out of her desperation to try to hold on to a husband and stop his philandering ways. All Whitney ever wanted was to love and be loved. I personally felt great pity and sadness for her, and yet she was the one who had the power to end her living nightmare. The episode resulted in another show cancellation. Nothing was ever again said about the hoped-for pregnancy, and it became a situation that simply had "never happened"; therefore, there was no cause to ever refer to it again.

As if that wasn't enough, the worst was yet to come. There was an incident that was so bloody heartbreaking for Whitney, and so secret, that there exists no written report or other reference on file.

For the 1994 US tour, we commenced our travels in June as a mobile daycare. To accompany Bobbi Kristina, Whitney generously allowed all her husband's other children, plus a few more youngsters, to travel with us free of charge. A teenage girl in the group, not one of Bobby Brown's children and somewhat older than the others, acted as a daytime nanny, keeping the children entertained while the working tour members did their thing. Thankfully, Bobby Brown's children did not stay with the tour through to the end. They all ultimately returned to their various mothers to commence their schooling commitments and so forth, leaving us to breathe a sigh of relief. The presence of so many young children caused an additional burden not only for security and tour management but for Aunt Bae as well, who acted as the mother superior and senior chaperone.

We were showing in Las Cruces, New Mexico, one evening when Silvia, Whitney's personal assistant, came to my hotel room. By this time Silvia and I had been through much together. We counted on one another for a helping hand and a kind ear. Reliable and caring, she had become a friend and a confidant. I could tell from her face that she was shaken, and I asked her what was the matter. She told me that the teenage girl who was serving as nanny to the kids had confided in her that earlier in the tour when she was coloring in a book alone in her hotel room, Bobby Brown entered looking for his children. He sat down and started coloring with her. She told Sylvia that he then raped her. She was now alleging she was pregnant. What bitter irony—while Whitney was convincing herself she was pregnant in an effort to hold on to her man, that same man was allegedly impregnating someone else. I asked Sylvia who else the girl had told. "Only me" was her response.

Laurie Badami was out shopping that afternoon, and Aunt Bae was not available for reasons that I can't recall. I was, of course, shocked at the allegations. As a policeman, that is how I saw it at the moment, as an uncorroborated and otherwise unsubstantiated allegation made by an underage girl against a male adult. It would have been inappropriate, and unprofessional, to reach any definitive conclusion.

I waited, trying to wrap my head around what I had been told and vacillating between shock and horror, and utter loathing and hatred. I found myself confronting a circumstance I had often dealt with as a police officer, but never in an instance so close to home.

I caught Laurie as she returned and was entering her room. In her doorway, I repeated what Silvia had told me. She dropped her shopping bags and fell to the floor. I thought she had suffered a bloody heart attack! But she had merely fainted.

I decided to phone John Houston. I gave him the news, stressing these were currently allegations without any form of corroboration or proof. His disgust and anger were palpable over the telephone, but now the legal wheels of the organization started to kick in.

To my utter horror, Whitney called me to her dressing room before the show and asked me to explain to her what I had told Laurie and what was going on. Only a few weeks had elapsed since her phantom pregnancy, and I was loath to give her more bad news. Why she needed affirmation from me, rather than those much closer to the issues, I will never know. I told her exactly what Silvia told me, what I repeated to Laurie, and a much-abbreviated version of what I had told her father, stressing above all else that it was an allegation, not a statement of fact. On completing my synopsis, she looked at me hard with cold eyes and simply said, "Thank you."

This incident abruptly ended what remained of the tour, an

unfortunate impact on everyone else, not to mention the fans who held tickets to shows yet to come. The very next morning, Whitney, Bobby, the baby, a few of the executive ladies, and I flew, quietly and soberly, by private jet back to the Morristown airport, where Whitney, Bobby, and the baby were picked up by Whitney's driver Tommy. Before departing the airfield, she again turned to me and said, "Thank you, David."

My heart felt heavy for her. They got in the vehicle and left for Mendham. That was the very last I or anyone else heard of what was one of the saddest events I had ever experienced with Whitney. She appeared heartbroken, but strangely resigned to it all.

Reportedly, the alleged victim and her mother were brought to North Gate in Mendham the next day, where they met with Whitney's legal team, John, and others of the inner circle. I do not know whether they had legal representation, but I doubt it. There simply had not been enough time for that. They were sent for, transported via plane, and driven to the residence. Suffice it to say, the matter was dealt with, and neither the girl nor the incident was ever discussed again. I mean *ever*.

Having had no opportunity to interview or even speak with the accuser, I was able to maintain a professional view that this was simply an allegation with no corroborative proof. I have no way of knowing whether the allegations were ultimately substantiated. But if the story was entirely without merit, then that raises the question *why?* Why would a young girl invent such a story? Could someone so young be so devious?

I will add here that two years after I parted ways with Whitney, I received a telephone call from a tour entourage member at my office in Morristown, New Jersey, alleging similar abuse by Bobby Brown with regard to the member's own daughter. The caller wanted a recommendation for a lawyer.

For the time being, though, Bobby Brown was still there, unscathed and carrying on as Whitney's loving husband. There had been no police involvement. Whitney appeared to have the ability to live with it, whatever the "it" was, which again shattered my judgment of her. I don't think it was a "forgive and forget" situation. She simply forgot something that never happened, at least in her mind. She believed what she needed to believe for her own peace of mind and ever-degenerating emotional stability.

I pondered how other women would have dealt with the situation—husband accused of raping of a minor, the minor reportedly pregnant as a result. Not a question I can answer personally. Whitney was surely a strong young woman. She had been and would continue to be obliged to endure more hurt than many, and all the time exposed to the public eye.

The universal familial dislike of her husband was nothing if not accentuated by the allegations. However, the tendency of all in the inner circle to clam up and place such things in an overloaded bin of indiscretions, to put it mildly, and then slam the lid shut, was astounding to me—and ultimately damaging to Whitney. The downward spiral was starting to rotate and gain momentum, and now everyone was beginning to suffer.

12

After Apartheid

And we moved on. Next up: South Africa. Apartheid having ended, we traveled there to commemorate and celebrate this truly historic event. Mandela had been elected president six months earlier, and Whitney was one of the first major musicians to visit. The One South Africa tour was sponsored by HBO, and our touring group was expanded to 250 people to include film crews and staff, plus an abundance of equipment. It was a massive logistical undertaking, and a massive security operation.

There were medical considerations—infectious diseases, insects, contaminated water. The recommended immunizations included polio, tetanus, typhoid, yellow fever, cholera, hepatitis A and B, meningococcal meningitis, rabies, tuberculosis, and the real teaser, schistosomiasis, a disease caused by a parasite that enters the body and lays eggs that last for years to come. By far the easiest way to contract these miserable maladies is through the bite of a mosquito, fly, flea, tick, or louse. Last on the list, but by no means least, was the old favorite, the tsetse fly, which can cause encephalitis—an inflammation of the brain—and "sleeping sickness."

My research through the Overseas Security Advisory Council (OSAC) and similar assessment entities revealed this sub-Saharan country to be a hotbed of crime and violence, with Johannesburg then having the distinction of being the murder capital of the world. The city was averaging fifty-two killings daily. Armed carjackers stole an average of sixty-five cars in Johannesburg every weekend; 80 percent of these carjackings were achieved with the use of firearms, the rest with knives or a combination of both. The incidence of crime had risen 30 percent since 1992. There were "no-go" zones for White people in the Witwatersrand townships on the East Rand outside Johannesburg.

I learned that violent and hostile groups could form with little or no warning, and innocent bystanders could easily find themselves victims. The situation was no better in Durban, with pickpockets targeting tourists, and muggers using extreme violence against any who resisted. Homicide in Durban was also becoming more prevalent, and considering that a gas-station robbery often entailed the use of grenades and AK-47s, the statistics became all the more daunting. American tourists had reported having stones thrown at their cars as they drove and their properties in affluent areas burglarized. The official line from the US embassy was to the effect that "adequate police response in the case of an emergency is doubtful." Cape Town appeared to be less of a risk in terms of crime and the potential for serious violence. Not a safe haven by any stretch of the imagination, but its morgue was not as busy as those in other major cities.

Into this environment, and in celebration of the end of apartheid, we were taking close to 250 US citizens in the entertainment industry, whose general perception of reality was naive at best. More of a necessity than ever before, tour manager Tony Bulluck headed our small team on a ten-day advance assessment visit, our first stop being Cape Town. The journey to South Africa was a miserable affair—some 17.5 hours' duration from New York, with a four-hour stop at Cape Verde airport—just a small hut actually—for an air crew change and refuel. I have never been able to sleep on planes, making this journey all the more dreadful.

On arrival we were hustled mercilessly by locals looking to earn rewards for providing a bag-carrying service, whether wanted or not, until being paid just to leave the arriving passengers alone. There was always the potential for them to simply grab the bag and run. Arthur Singer, our travel agent, was immediately badgered and assaulted by a hustler who insisted on taking his bags, fighting violently to relieve him of his suitcase, with poor Arthur hanging on to it for dear life until I intervened and suitably encouraged the would-be porter to let go and clear off. We were told that carrying a stick was useful to ward off these hordes of opportunists preying on visitors entering the country. Taking the advice, I acquired and carried a heavy carved ebony walking cane, to be used as a cudgel, if needed, more than as an ambulatory aid.

As we entered the hotel, a hustler tried to approach a vehicle at the entrance and was stopped by the doorman. The hustler promptly stubbed out a cigarette on the doorman's hand. Within ten minutes of two guards allowing us entry to the hotel, those same guards were beaten by striking security guards outside the front door, apparently for crossing their picket line. Later in the day the police fought running battles in the street using tear gas and rubber bullets to disperse a crowd that had appeared out of nowhere.

Our first time on the continent, we assessed hitherto unchartered territory and dangers with trepidation. Preparations included acquiring bullet-resistant clothing and engaging one of the foremost security teams in South Africa at the time, an organization run by a British citizen named Mike Middlemass, then a long-term resident in South Africa. His advice to me on landing and handing me a pistol was "Mr. Roberts, in the event of having to use this, shoot first, we'll ask questions later."

We visited many of the show locations on our schedule. Mike's team of professionals, which included former and current police officers, would provide in-locus security in all our intended ports of call—Durban, Johannesburg, and Cape Town. I had anticipated that the Cape Town Green Point Stadium would be our easiest venue, and so it was with resigned disappointment that I learned that at a recent UB40 concert there, five hundred firearms had been confiscated from attending fans. Vehicles, drivers, and ancillary backup personnel, all armed, would remain with us throughout our tour, with the exception of the "royal" visit to Swaziland, where we were scheduled to meet with a king and his many wives. A rare treat indeed.

As I became more familiar with the environment, and in being escorted around learning routes and alternatives to and from the various venues with Mike and his team, I was shocked to see suburban homes protected not simply by barbed and razor wire, but by electrified fencing on top of castle-like walls. Whitney's longtime friend Robyn had accompanied us on the pretour. She told me that she was obliged to run from one location she was surveying for potential press conference purposes, being chased by crowds wanting a share in the wealth she enjoyed and that was obvious to them by her dress and demeanor.

She was boldly considering a press conference to be held at Vista University in Soweto, notwithstanding the fact we had been advised that the South African press are considerably worse than their English counterparts, and that was saying something. The impression we were given was that the local media were even more disgusting and intrusive than those in Copenhagen, and that, in my opinion, would be nigh on impossible. When we were there, the Danish media had taken great delight in entering Whitney's suite and taking photographs of the unmade bed in which she and her husband had been sleeping, and then published those photos for the edification and sexual gratification of their readers. They made the US gutter media look honorable by comparison.

There was also good reason to believe that those in authority at the airport, promising all manner of secure communication and unencumbered travel to us, were in fact working in cahoots with and on the payroll of their media associates. It became clear we would more likely than not be compromised at every juncture, regardless of promised security protocols. Soweto, the vast shantytown location of so much civil disobedience and violence, did end up being Robyn's choice of venue for Whitney's press conference. In fairness, Robyn was being overtly manipulated by Zindzi Mandela, one of the daughters of the great Nelson Mandela. Zindzi ran some form of marketing/media entity and was clearly corrupt, as were many of the other so-called officials we were bound to deal with for this trip. Zindzi was preparing what looked to me like a potentially hazardous itinerary for Whitney's exposure, which included a walkabout in Soweto. Trying to get her to confirm that itinerary was like pulling teeth without anesthesia: very bloody painful.

Many officials there viewed Whitney and her entourage simply as a source for exploitation and an opportunity for their own self-serving purposes and financial gain. It was quite depressing to watch, especially as certain members of our executive party were so intent on fawning, pandering, and bending over backward to ingratiate themselves with this new Black South African world that they could not see the obvious. Even then, it was plain that one of our greatest security vulnerabilities would be that our group was overwhelmed with the idea of returning to the land of their ancestors, and as such were blindly placing themselves at great risk. It also became clear that, as a White man, my estimations of such a weakness were not going to be well received. Yet my perspective was that greed and overt exploitation seeped through the very core of what should have been a celebratory event.

Furthermore, the music and concert industry in South Africa was in deep trouble. Big Concerts, a promotions entity responsible for bringing in world-class music acts like the Rolling Stones and Sting, was reportedly hopelessly insolvent. According to an article in the

Sunday Times, it was some 6 million rand in debt. That we were involved with Big Concerts was troubling, but at least we now had advance knowledge and the lawyers would take over and, with luck, control any issues that might arise.

Courtesy of the introduction of Mike and his team, the local police were excellent in their intent to provide whatever assistance they could. I visited the Johannesburg Central Police Station, formerly the much-feared John Vorster Square detention center, and met with a police chief on the upper floor of one of its buildings. There I was shown a door through which it was reported, somewhat tongue-in-cheek, that prisoners were led after interrogation and released. On opening the door, however, I was shocked to see it led directly outside the building with no steps. In other words, the only way down was free fall from a height of ten floors up. It was said jokingly, perhaps, but given the past reputation and allegations regarding police brutality in dealing with the African National Congress, one had to wonder why there would be a fire escape door at that level with no obvious means of exiting except being thrown or pushed.

Many people accompanied us on the South Africa trip, not because they were needed, but because Whitney invited them. Two of those people were ANITA BAXTER, an outside vendor who worked with Whitney, and her husband. Whitney and Bobby would sometimes "escape" to stay with the Baxters at their beach house, so Anita, and by extension her husband, tended to have the ability and authority to travel with us, and it was always with an air of implied importance.

Shortly before our first show at King Park Stadium in the city of Durban, I was called to the car park of our hotel by our security team, where reportedly there was a serious problem in progress. When I got there the local security driver, a police officer, pointed to the

limousine where Mr. Baxter was seated. He had commissioned our
limousine, got in, and demanded that the driver take him into the
city to buy drugs. The driver was refusing to accommodate Baxter's
criminal demands, and rightly so.

I approached Mr. Baxter and said, "You have just asked a police
officer to take you into town to buy drugs. The only place this officer
will take you is to his police station. Your choice—sit there and be
arrested, or get out of the fucking car now." I thought his eyes were
going to fall out of his head. The prospect of spending time in a
South African jail put an end to his quest to buy drugs. He shot out
of the car and vanished back into the hotel.

I apologized to the driver and Mike, and we all had a good laugh.
Baxter's face had been a picture when he realized who he was asking
to break the law. I reported it to Tony Bulluck and the management
team, and to be honest, I cannot remember seeing Baxter again on that
tour. After that, the appearance and presence of Anita Baxter would
forever leave a bad taste in my mouth, with associated deep concerns
as to her real purpose and value to Whitney, beyond relieving her of
money for one nefarious service or another.

The morning after our show in Durban, I was in my hotel room
typing up my security briefing for the day—warnings for the staff of
the particular dangers and perils they could face. I always made sure
everyone knew exactly what to expect, where everything was, and
what issues they would need to contend with at a given venue. The
executive party was on the upper floors with Big Bob and the security
team, while I had a cabana at ground level, with a small front garden
elevated above and a few yards from the ocean. I was typing away
when I was startled by a loud noise right outside my front door, the
unmistakable crack of a gunshot. I stepped out of the room to see

crowds running away from the ledge outside my cabana toward the sandy beach.

I approached the site everyone was anxious to leave and looked over the edge. At the foot of the wall, lying in the sand about six feet below me, was the body of a well-dressed White woman. A large section of her head was missing, brain matter splattered against the sea wall as she sat with her back propped against it. A gun lay by her side, her blouse drenched in blood, its metallic smell wafting through the air, overwhelming that of the gunpowder. My heart leapt when I saw the short blonde spiked hair on what was left of her head. She had the look, size, and weight of Lynne Volkman, one of our executives. I thought that maybe the body was hers, though I had no idea how or why she would have acquired a firearm. The police arrived on scene and quickly established the identity of the South African woman through the contents of a wallet found on the body.

I returned to the cabana and was later told that the woman was so depressed by the end of apartheid that she had decided to end her life rather than alter her lifestyle to accommodate the equality of Black people in it. Apparently she was not an isolated case, according to the police. I learned that many Whites left South Africa due to the (not entirely unjustified) fear of (also not entirely unjustified) retribution. Others left for racist reasons; they simply had no desire to live under a South Africa governed by its overwhelmingly Black majority. Some left because they didn't want their artificially boosted standards of living to change. The end of apartheid would mean that Whites would have less available to them and more competition. For these reasons many left, and as I witnessed firsthand, some committed suicide.

I wondered whether this unique period of change for South Africa was ever going to work. Then I had the honor of meeting the man who provided some confidence that an orderly transition was possible—Nelson Mandela.

From Durban we traveled to Johannesburg, where the hotel management had expressed the opinion that no White person, or really any tourist of any color, should go out into the city streets by themselves unless accompanied by assigned hotel security guards. In fact, the situation was so dire that the security warnings to tour personnel were simple—do not leave the confines of our hotel, other than to travel to and from venues under armed protection. Suffice it to say that while I am very familiar with body armor, Johannesburg is the only place in the world where I have worn both a bullet-resistant undershirt vest and a protected windbreaker-style jacket at the same time.

Our show at Ellis Park Arena in Johannesburg sold out its one-hundred-thousand-person capacity. There again, so smitten and blinded were some of our tour members that they placed Whitney in a position of compromise when she was advised to announce onstage that Winnie Madikizela-Mandela, the second wife of the president, was the "Queen of South Africa." Whitney was seldom booed onstage in those days, but with the South African White people, and more than a few Black people, having a somewhat alternative view of the criminal that was Winnie Mandela, their united displeasure was a forgone conclusion. Known to have ordered kidnappings, torture, and murders and for her support of "necklacing" (burning victims alive with a tire around the neck), she was denounced for her human rights violations in the name of the struggle against apartheid, and was certainly not considered a queen by many, to put it mildly.

Nelson Mandela attended the show in Johannesburg in person, and there was an emotional exchange between Whitney and Mr. Mandela. Cissy Houston stood on one side and every face of our entourage crammed into the background, forging an image to be a matter of public record for eternity. The moment Mandela turned to wipe a tear from Whitney's eye will forever be held as precious by many.

On National Defence Force Day, we had occasion to visit personally with Nelson Mandela at his official residence and office
at Mahlamba Ndlopfu in Bryntirion, Pretoria. We accompanied
Whitney and her family into the presidential offices and, after
Whitney and Bobby had a private audience with him, the great
man came into the anteroom and shook all of our hands. When
he came to Big Bob, he commented on his size in awed yet jocular
terms—"My, you're a big one!" and we all had a great laugh with
him. I am certain Bob will remember that very special moment for
the rest of his life.

I still cannot help but seethe with loathing when I recount the events
that took place after the show in Johannesburg. With the thrill of
Whitney's encounter with Mandela still buzzing, the entire entourage
was enjoying a relaxing after-show moment in the hotel, drinking and
laughing, and generally having a great time. As the evening wore on,
Bobby Brown declared he wanted Kentucky Fried Chicken, knowing that there was one such fast-food, heart attack–inducing eatery
on the so-called Killing Street of Central Johannesburg. The local
security team was mortified and intimated that this was something
that could not, under any circumstances, be done safely. Bobby
pressed. The security team offered to send some of the Black team
members to acquire an order. No! Bobby insisted he wanted to go,
and Whitney wanted to go with him. They felt they were "home" in
the land of their ancestors; they were indestructible on their native
African turf and no harm could possibly befall them. Discussions
and pleadings regarding the exposure to compromise, the threat
to everyone's well-being, and the potential for serious injury (or
worse) all fell on deaf ears. Bobby insisted on being taken to make
the purchase himself, and Whitney, especially exhilarated after the

stunning events of the past few days, insisted on going with him. I managed to acquire a few minutes to prepare the security teams for the dangerous task ahead.

Our entourage of vehicles left to visit one of the most crime-ridden and dangerous environments in the country. In his usual bombastic manner, Bobby bounced out of the vehicle and into the restaurant, Whitney in tow. At that time of night very few people were visible in the dark recesses of the street in question. Once inside, Bobby started his usual *Look at me folks, I'm here*, and Whitney played along, as she often did, to match him. Within seconds, people started showing up. Not just a few people, dozens of people. And then hundreds. It was easy to see how spontaneous riots of excessive numbers could crop up in seconds flat. They were not just ambling or walking to where we were parked but running en masse.

The KFC and our vehicles were surrounded by a jostling crowd, all of whom wanted a piece of the action. If we didn't act immediately, we would be in serious trouble. I grabbed the bucket of chicken wings from Bobby and ordered the two of them back in the vehicle. "No arguments from you. Get in the fucking car now!" They knew this was turning into a mob like they had never before experienced. We got in line behind the lead vehicle, with a backup vehicle to our rear, and started driving into and through the crowd as it physically pressed into the cars, rocking them back and forth with more and more people pushing up against the windows. Some of our local team got out to clear a route. They were overwhelmed by the crowd but still managed to facilitate a means whereby we could drive out of the street. The principals looked petrified.

In a perverse way I felt wholly satisfied, and totally vindicated. Bobby and Whitney created real fear and danger for themselves and others by thinking all this was some sort of game; by believing I was exaggerating the dangers and attempting to inhibit their fun; by mistakenly believing that the color of their skin would protect them.

They did not understand that it was the color of their money, not their skin, that motivated those who had nothing, not even hope.

The look on Bobby's face was classic and unforgettable: scared shitless. But still, knowing the real danger he had placed everyone in—especially his wife—all for the sake of a stupid bucket of KFC wings, he was not even remotely remorseful. He did not apologize to us. No one did, and by now I was well versed in giving them the "I told you so" look, with no expectation of an acknowledgment of fault. The ironic icing on the cake? The next morning the damned bucket of congealed KFC wings sat outside the door of their hotel room, hardly touched.

The selfish and wanton disregard Bobby had for others, though often evident, had never been so clearly illustrated. It took a long time for my anger to subside, and because I had very little respect for the man to start with, there was little of that to lose. I apologized to our local team. Their feelings toward Bobby more than mirrored my own and that of my team. Some of the Black members of the South African security team reasoned that Bobby and people like him were the precise reason apartheid lasted as long as it did. It was an understandable reaction under the circumstances, and by people who had been brought up with and lived through it all. I would not argue with it. I had too much respect for those offering the opinions, after they had been needlessly placed in harm's way.

In the afternoon on November 5, we went on a walkabout in Soweto, one of the saddest places I had ever seen. We visited the Blackchain supermarket, Baragwanath Hospital, the Orlando Power Station, Vista University, the Soweto Teachers' Training College, and the Soweto squatter settlement. We also visited Mandela's old residence and the home of Archbishop Desmond Tutu.

The kids rushed out to see Whitney and we kept a loose perimeter to try to control the crowds, but had any of them had a malevolent intent, we would have been helpless against them. It was a nerve-racking couple of hours for the security team, and I for one was extremely grateful that despite the unbridled and endearing zeal of the children, we managed to extricate ourselves unscathed. The local security team took big breaths when that was over.

We visited a children's school, and a singing competition where there was enthusiasm for signing up some young South Africans to Whitney's production company. Many promises were made, but I never again saw that talent on our travels and do not know if any such promises materialized for the youngsters. Much of the proceeds of Whitney's tour in South Africa was to be dispersed among children's homes, schools, and hospitals, but I personally wondered how much of that money was eaten up as "expenses" by those who had been entrusted with the task.

———————

We took some relaxation time at Sun City Resort, a luxury resort and casino situated in the North West Province between the Elands River and the Pilanesberg, about 140 kilometers northwest of Johannesburg. We stayed at the unique Palace of the Lost City, with a layout and architecture that was quite awesome. We all enjoyed the break, there being no incidents of any significance to mar the stay, with Whitney and Bobby taking the time to rest and simply relax. The game reserve tour was perhaps somewhat lackluster: all we saw were an ailing wart-hog and the carcass of a dead elephant being eaten by vultures.

In total contrast to the enjoyment of the resort, we also visited the small landlocked country of Swaziland. Exiting our plane—a typical Fred Flintstone model where one had to trust that the propellers wouldn't fall off—my first confrontation was with an individual purporting to be the head of security for the king. He demanded to travel in the car with my principal. He was denied, much to his obvious displeasure, but there was no way this reportedly Libyan-trained and armed bodyguard with dubious hygiene habits was getting close to my principals. He angrily left to follow in a car with the rest of his chums. We were deposited at a pit of a hotel with limited working amenities, purportedly the best "luxury" hotel in the country. HOLIDAY INN was imprinted on the postage stamp–sized soaps provided.

We were told that the 130-plus wives and offspring in the royal family were housed in another hotel-like structure that looked to me like a prison. For me, dealing with one wife at a time had proven difficult enough, but 130 all at once? To meet the king and a selection of his most esteemed wives, we were expected to get on our hands and knees and crawl through the dust into a vast grass-covered hut, wherein we were to bow and fawn to his royal highness. Being dressed in a suit, I declined the invitation and happily stayed outside while all others, Whitney and Bobby included, got down on all fours to get inside. Had I gone in, the king's head of security would have enjoyed my presence in his personal domain where his superiority over me would be at play. Such was the pissing contest of sorts that had quickly been established between the two of us. However, he seemed happy despite this missed opportunity on his part.

While it was an unforgettable experience, I was relieved to return home where I could let down my guard. South Africa had been by far the most taxing destination I had traveled to in terms of directing security and keeping everyone safe. And with that, the Bodyguard World Tour, covering 5 continents, 21 countries, and 120 concerts, and lasting 502 days, finally came to an end. Bobbi Kristina, now a walking and babbling little toddler, had been a tiny four-month-old lump of gurgling sweetness when we began. We had been around the world multiple times, and Whitney had shot into the outermost atmosphere of stardom.

13

Silence of the Stars

There were a number of times over the years when Whitney would take off for a few days in search of some respite from the rigors of touring. When she wanted to escape, truly relax, think, and receive guidance and comfort when troubled, she would reach out to CeCe Winans. Whitney and I would travel to Tennessee for a few days, where she would stay in CeCe's home with her family, and I'd be in a local hotel.

BeBe and CeCe Winans, who sang as both solo artists and a brother-sister duo, are well known in the gospel world, with numerous albums to their credit. They both shared a profound and special friendship with Whitney, who looked up to and heavily relied on CeCe for emotional support. Their brother, Pastor Marvin Winans, was the one who married Whitney and Bobby. CeCe was truly not only a beautiful woman on the outside but also one of the most beautiful-hearted individuals on the face of God's earth. I enjoyed those trips, especially because I could see how they nourished Whitney, something she needed so desperately at times.

The respite Whitney sought in January 1995 was of a different sort, in that Bobby was with us. Whitney, Bobby, the baby, Aunt

Bae's daughter Shelly, Whitney's personal assistant Silvia, and I left a hectic L.A. schedule to fly by private jet to Telluride, Colorado. We were greeted at the airport by limousines, and we enjoyed the twenty-minute ride through the countryside to get to the spa, passing many notable mansions. Oprah Winfrey had one on a slope from which, our guide told us, she could ski down into the town of Telluride. As it had been a spontaneous decision and characterized as a day trip, I was attired entirely inappropriately. I could handle being cold for a day, but equally spontaneously, "we" decided to remain for longer. We checked into a boutique hotel known as the Peaks at the base of the San Juan Mountains, where all the world's fashionistas and bejeweled studs could be seen strutting their stuff unabashedly. Upon arrival, Whitney and crew attended the renowned hotel spa, the original purpose of the day trip, giving me time to get to the gift shop and purchase some suitable cold-weather clothing.

The next day Whitney and Bobby went skiing. I did not know one end of a ski from another, so I accompanied them to the slopes wearing boots only. They rented their equipment from the store in the hotel and off we went. My method was to hurtle down the snowy slopes on foot and at an ever-escalating pace dictated more by gradient and gravity than any running prowess on my part. I was actually quicker than both of them but had to stop many times to pick up the fallen duo, neither of whom appeared to know any more about skiing than I did. We had a lot of fun. Back at the lodge we warmed up in front of a fireplace as big as the living room of my apartment, containing burning logs as big as trees.

After another afternoon at the spa, dinner at the restaurant, and an early evening, Whitney phoned my room and asked me to accompany her husband to the town of Telluride so he could have a drink. I was mortified, but anticipating my reaction, she quickly followed with assurances that she and the ladies would be perfectly safe and not venture out of their rooms, so I did not have to worry. I wasn't so sure. She was more concerned that Bobby was "looked after." To me that meant I should make sure he didn't get into trouble.

So off he and I went, eagerly on his part, as he had been under matrimonial constraints too long, and reluctantly on my part. We arrived at a local pub, well attended by many wealthy, young, beautiful women clad in designer winter outfits. Bobby and I sat at a table and chatted about nothing in particular. Then he got up and said he was going to buy another drink for us. Watching him talk with people at the bar, I had a sinking feeling in the pit of my stomach. He came back to the table and left me a beer, saying that he was just going to the bar to continue a conversation with a girl he had met there. I told him not to go out of my sight. He nodded his assent, which translated meant *Yeah, right!* There were many such moments between Bobby and me.

After a while, the conversation and drinks clearly going down exceptionally well, judging by the body language and mutual interaction, Bobby came back to the table and said he was just going outside with the girl and would be back in a few minutes. Oh hell. Another *Yeah, right!* He never came back. I went outside to search. Nothing. Nowhere to be found. So I left and went back to the hotel. He was a grown man and perfectly capable of looking after himself.

The next morning brought with it a telephone call from the police. Bobby was being accused of sexual assault and harassment, presumably by the woman with whom he had left the bar, and the police were looking to interview him. A few telephone calls later, and we had a local criminal defense attorney involved and taking control of the situation. Ultimately, this "little problem," like so many others, was handled through skilled and persuasive negotiation, and the San Miguel County district attorney's office decided not to prosecute. It went away with no more ado.

We kept a very low profile that day. Stayed in our rooms. Despite having been born in the shadow of the mountains of Wales, and later working there, it was only after I spent long hours just waiting and looking out the window of the hotel in Colorado that I realized mountains have a life unto themselves. The shapes and colors change constantly, a phenomenon of nature caused by the sun and its constant trajectory across the sky, intermittently hidden and transformed by passing clouds. A shift that would change flat to craggy, safe areas to dangerous ones. Sitting there, I watched a projection of the uncertain and ever-changing nature of life itself. The entire visual experience summoned a perfect metaphor for our lives on the road together.

The extended day trip to Telluride extended still further, and the next morning saw Whitney, Bobby, and me off to a horseback riding excursion in one of the valleys. It had been arranged for a local cowboy to take the two riding for a couple of hours. I hate horses. Having been double-kicked by a pony on my uncle's farm as a boy, and having been a part of and seen the damage these beasts can do during riot control while serving as a police officer at New Scotland Yard, I had a healthy respect for the animals. And an even healthier desire to ensure the greatest distance possible between them and me.

I hoped that I could leave Bobby and Whitney to ride the range romantically and alone with the cowboy. But my heart sank when Bobby approached his horse, turned around, and announced that he didn't like the animal and was going back to the hotel bar. We could find him there on our return. Clearly still smarting from what I suspected had been a berating at the hands of Whitney, John Houston, Whitney's attorney Sheldon, and others for his gross indiscretion with the alleged Telluride assault victim, he was ready to put great distance between himself and anyone who would give him grief. That being said, Whitney did not seem to mind seeing him go, albeit perhaps troubled by the "I'm going to the bar" remark. She simply turned to me and said, "Then you and I will ride, David."

Unlike me, Whitney was very enthusiastic about the adventure. I was not sure whether she had any experience with horses, but there were times when this woman knew no fear. This, unfortunately for me, was clearly going to be one of those times. She mounted her steed handily. The cowboy then gave a boost to my resisting body, and I clambered onto the gigantic wild beast that appeared not at all fazed by my shaking presence on his back. As I squeezed his ribs with all my might, I remained healthily skeptical, especially as Whitney's mare seemed a little frisky.

The cowboy flew into his saddle like it was metal and he had magnets in the seat of his pants. And we were off at what to me was a breakneck speed, but what was in reality a slow trudge. Whitney was thrilled, all the more so because she could see that I was somewhat, shall we say, uncomfortable (read: petrified). From where I sat, the creature may well have been a dragon—any second flames would surely shoot from the animal's nostrils, and we'd shoot into the atmosphere. After a bit, I settled down somewhat, at which point the cowboy and Whitney, sensing that I was beginning to feel comfortable, my eyes back in my sockets and my knuckles no longer white, decided we should canter.

For the love of God Almighty! I started bouncing in the saddle, trying to emulate how I had seen others ride, sort of timing my ups and downs to the motion of the horse. And doing it badly. I was getting pummeled in the backside. I silently cursed Bobby for his stubborn petulance in putting me through this sheer agony, as he should have been the one bouncing his balls off and I should have been the one waiting at the bar. From a canter, we revved up to a bloody gallop. I say *bloody* not so much as an expletive, but more as an adjective to describe my backside, as by this time I had every confidence that the blood vessels there were surely ruptured and must be bleeding through.

After what, for Whitney, was clearly an exhilarating experience, we came down to a slow walk. Eminently more manageable. Although by then, there was temporarily no feeling whatsoever in my nether region and I suspected that part of my body had simply died. We rode through some of the most stunning scenery I have ever seen in my life. A vast blue sky dotted with gleaming clouds seemed to pull thoughts from your head and send them reverberating across the valley. We looked out through the crisp air at a green expanse ringed by soaring snow-capped peaks. In the rustle of the grass, the snap of a twig, the gurgle of a mountain stream, and the swish of a horse's tail, life was all around us. Pure life. Clean life. Ancient and enduring life. It was a setting ripe for contemplation. Whitney and I talked.

She was worried about Bobby and events like the latest nonsense. She was not looking for answers. She wanted someone to listen, and who better than her trusted bodyguard? I gave her the sounding board she wanted, offering nothing more than comfort and acknowledgment. As we proceeded, having got a load off her chest, she turned to me in her saddle and said, "David, I'm thinking of buying a place out here and moving. Would you come with me?"

I was flabbergasted. Come with her—try stopping me! Once again, in probably misplaced spontaneous British semi-Shakespearean fashion, and hoping my leaping and thumping heart did not give me away, I responded, "Whither thou goest, my lady, so shall I always follow."

She burst out laughing. She got it and she liked it.

In that moment, in that serene and majestic setting, a new and deeper bond was cemented between protectee and protector. She knew that nothing would ever happen to her or her daughter on my watch. I imagined the rest of my working life would never be more than a few feet away from this incredibly beautiful and talented young woman, and that was precisely what I wanted. I allowed myself to picture it, allowed my heart to fill.

———

The ride came to an end and our cowboy dismounted in a single smooth movement, helped Whitney slide deftly off her horse, and then came to assist me clumsily off my long-suffering steed. Holy God above! When my feet hit terra firma, I realized I could not put my knees together. More than that, it felt as if a vast wedge had been rammed between my arse cheeks and my hips had simply parted. The pain was excruciating, and Whitney and our cowboy were totally amused by my—somewhat feigned and exaggerated for effect—performance. I have found in my life that there's always time for a sense of humor, even in adverse conditions, and I exploit those occasions without compunction.

By the time the limousine took us back to the hotel, the pain had subsided, but I played along, moaning and complaining, simply for the pure fun of it all, and to lighten the rather dark ambience created by Bobby's most recent indiscretion. It worked, as people love a good laugh at the expense of another, especially people who are experiencing their own troubles. Bobby was indeed at the bar and, regaled by Whitney, enjoyed the story of my challenges with horsemanship. I daresay she never did mention the desired move to Colorado, but this was not Bobby Brown country. She knew that, too, which made me think perhaps she was considering some major changes in her life, to include unburdening herself of certain loads that were proving too heavy to carry.

Another spa session that afternoon for them and one more surprise for the evening: snowmobiles up to an abandoned mine some eleven thousand feet above sea level. Who in the hell thought of these never-ending special diversions for us? Our entourage left the hotel in the dead of night. Whitney and Bobby shared a snowmobile, I had my own, and the tour guides and others rode several more. We zoomed off across the frozen plains, icy air and snow spray whipping our masked and goggled faces. Going higher and higher into the Rockies, we followed a path to the very gates of heaven, it seemed to me.

We arrived at a village by the name of Alta, a tiny ghost town with an abandoned mine and the remnants of shacks where miners had lived. When we turned off the clattering and whining snowmobile engines, we experienced a treat of sight and sound beyond compare. The sound was pure silence, a silence so profound it was almost overwhelming. The sight was the sky above, crystal clear and as black as black could be. The stars, so many of them—the entire Milky Way and galaxies beyond—so close it felt that if I extended my hand upward to the heavens, I could take a finger and jostle them about.

14

Too Good to Be White

We moved on to Whitney's second film: *Waiting to Exhale*. Based on Terry McMillan's novel about four friends, there was no perceived conflict with my presence on the set, as there had been with *The Bodyguard*. This one was mine to look after. I even acquired a mention in the rolling credits at the end of the film.

After considerable preparations and significant interaction with yet another facet of the entertainment industry, in February 1995 we all moved to Phoenix, Arizona, for this new adventure. The staff were housed in an extended-stay residence hotel where we each had our own little apartment with a bedroom, bathroom, living room, and kitchenette. Whitney had rented a private residence a few miles from the hotel, where she stayed with Aunt Bae, Aunt Bae's daughter Shelly, Whitney's assistant Silvia, and Bobbi Kristina. From a security perspective, I was not especially happy with the arrangement, but they hired a vehicle for my personal use and I was confident that I could respond quickly in an emergency. The reasoning for the distancing was that Whitney needed some "self-time" during the filming process, given the pressures she was under and had recently endured on tour.

The local police were excellent, exceptionally discreet, and helpful. We developed a good system of responses in the event of a problem, and it was with some confidence that I planned the security protocols for the numerous film sets. Within forty-eight hours of setup at the residence and hotel, we were good to go from a security perspective. Tommy, Whitney's chauffeur, would drive the principal's vehicle, I would drive backup, and off we would go to collect Whitney, as per her day's schedule, for filming.

There were some wonderful people on the set with Whitney. A great working relationship was quickly achieved with the actors and crew. One evening, after a shoot, Whitney asked me to take her costar Angela Bassett back to her residence. She is an absolutely delightful lady. It was a rare treat indeed for me to interact with her, even though we became momentarily lost in the streets of Phoenix searching for her hotel.

As the early-start days extended into long nights, I began to understand how exploitative the film industry was of those anxious to become a part of it in any capacity. The kids doing the dirty jobs were so keen to participate, their enthusiasm knew no bounds and was consistent from start to finish. From what I recall, the only issues that arose were related to the extras, who would stand around for ten hours waiting for a three-minute filming session and who were not as professionally attuned to their roles as the crew was. It was occasionally an issue keeping them from seeking autographs and so forth.

Often the assembling of sets was complicated by the special lighting requirements associated with filming Black actors, something I had never considered. There were frequent delays between reshooting a scene, especially outdoors with the sun constantly moving. And in Arizona the sun shines a lot. During inside shoots, by far the longest element was the setting up of lighting. I was singularly impressed with the personal industry and drive that motivated these competitive young people, and how they were mentored and encouraged to push themselves harder by more seasoned staff who still had an astounding enthusiasm for what they did best.

The film was directed by Forest Whitaker, whom I found to be a very nice chap. He and I share the same birthday, although I am some nine years his senior. His directing experience was limited at the time, although his character portrayals as an actor had earned him accolades. There was some blowback from those who opined that the film should have been directed by a woman. But I observed Mr. Whitaker to be a hardworking, dedicated, and uniquely focused professional. I do remember pondering, however, whether he was perhaps out of his depth in undertaking such a project. Not only was it his first time directing a major film, but he also had to deal with the likes of the Whitney Houston Machine, with all its demands, peculiarities, and contract stipulations. Those were elements expected from a touring singer of her repute, though of the performers on the set she was the least experienced in the acting discipline, which perhaps created a modicum of resentment in the "real" actors. I never heard this said out loud, but the odd rolling of eyes and exasperated breaths gave hints. In fairness, we posed a challenge to any environment we entered and in which we moved.

Our traveling party comprised Laurie Badami, Silvia Vejar, Tommy Wattley, Aunt Bae, Shelly Long for Bobbi Kristina, Carol Ensminger for hair in general, and Ellin LaVar as a set hairdresser. Completing the permanent film entourage was Whitney's longtime and well-traveled makeup artist, a personality known as Quietfire. He spent much of his downtime with Wendy Wiseman, Whitney's masseuse, and Roberta Quick, who provided security for the baby.

Robyn would visit from time to time, bringing on pains for Laurie, who was becoming repulsed by the mere presence of Robyn in our midst. Ever since Laurie had replaced her, Robyn took pleasure in seeing Laurie fail in her duties. Robyn's desire to see Laurie fail was wearing on Laurie. The animosity between the two increased as Laurie sunk deeper into dysfunction and emotional distress. Actually, it was becoming clear that Laurie was losing it completely.

Bobby Brown would visit from time to time as well, seriously contributing to Laurie's personal problems because he would take off with Laurie's boyfriend, Tommy Wattley. The two of them would get involved in heaven knows what, for however long it took, which enraged Laurie. As I saw it, Tommy was a free spirit in the truest sense of the term, and not one to be tied down, restricted, or emotionally controlled in any way. Ever.

Bobby was likewise inclined, but at that time Whitney actually encouraged Bobby to get lost with Tommy. She had no time for him. The other difference was that Bobby and Whitney were married, and Tommy and Laurie were not. That seemed to breed an insidious insecurity in Laurie that grew daily into a malignancy infecting her emotional state—a poisonous situation as time on the set passed. Further, Tommy seemed to feel the entrapment of being so closely tied to Laurie's apron strings. Unlike in New York, his home turf, in Phoenix he effectively had nowhere to escape from the group in general, and Laurie in particular, other than when Bobby was in town and they would promptly disappear. And then later, he would be lambasted by her for it.

―――――――――――――

There were some enjoyable moments in Arizona. On one occasion I accompanied Whitney shopping at the local mall. As we happily progressed through the clothing section of one store, she was recognized by a young Black girl who, quite simply, froze and started to scream uncontrollably. I managed to quiet the child down—big breaths, big breaths. Whitney was gracious as ever, and the girl crumpled into gasping silence and then tears when Whitney comforted her. No crowd formed and we were good to go. I was glad to get us out of that one. Whitney and I laughed about it later.

During that period, I acquired a new Ruger .380—a small yet effective concealment weapon—and Whitney and I practiced protocols for any time that the use of a firearm would be necessary to protect and save her life. One such drill contemplated her being grabbed from behind and held. On my signal, she would kick back at the legs of the attacker and then throw her torso forward, allowing her body weight to unbalance him for sufficient time for me to apply a double tap (two consecutive shots fired at speed) to the exposed top of head, shoulders, or spine, depending on the reaction of the assailant to the sudden change of weight distribution. If the attacker opened their arms to allow Whitney to fall, she would be on the way down and the attacker would be left standing and exposed. Same protocol, double tap to the central body mass of the torso. Tommy played the attacker on one occasion, and it proved to Whitney that the protocol would work. This gave us both confidence in one another, and in the execution of the plan, as I would need her to act in a certain way under the extremes of pressure.

The first cracks in the facade of our supposedly loving and caring family unit came when a serious issue developed between Quietfire and Ellin LaVar. The two were competing hairdressers and makeup artists serving Whitney at varying times, but seldom together. In a nutshell, Ellin hated Quietfire, and that hatred, though often not visible as they seldom worked together, was a sure sign of the growing rot yet to affect us all. Meanwhile, Tommy and Laurie's relationship ebbed and flowed, and the arguments and fights escalated in seriousness. There were three occasions when they "split" and sought separate hotel rooms. A couple of these splits were so disruptive that hotel officials had to get involved.

Whitney had a belly full of them all: Tommy and Laurie's domestic ongoing crisis, interpersonal bickering and arguing, family back in New Jersey, Bobby's ever-present comings and goings, media stories regarding his excesses, and so forth. At the end of one day's filming, she ignored all of them as they waited in her car. She got into mine and sat next to me.

"Drive, David. Just drive. I've had enough of these fools today."

I drove, following Tommy and everyone else in the lead vehicle, the occupants tentatively looking back to see what was going on between Whitney and me. Then Whitney said, "Turn here!" It was a left turn off the main drag. I did as she commanded. She had seen them ahead and picked the perfect moment to leave them behind completely. The shocked look on the faces of those in the lead vehicle was classic. Tommy had committed to driving beyond the turn I had taken in his wake, and they could do nothing but continue their journey back to the residence.

Whitney did not talk. She visibly relaxed and within a short time was dozing in the seat next to me. I slowed to facilitate her ability to relax and rest. It was another one of those special moments between us. She was at peace—at least for that one moment in time. She felt safe with me. When we arrived at the house, there they all were, looking accusingly at me and, like scolded children, seeking approval from Whitney. She just smiled. She had them all over a barrel.

Things did not improve. I knew something was terribly amiss when I received a fax from Tony Bulluck regarding the forthcoming Brunei tour. Some five days previous he had requested a response to some important issue from Laurie and had received none. Likewise, Laurie had failed to let Whitney know that that Toni Chambers was no longer John Houston's assistant. It seemed there were troubles beyond just our enclave.

Laurie ultimately came to me and admitted she could no longer perform her functions for Whitney. She stated that she had failed to respond to all messages requesting action by her. She was then at least seven days behind where she should have been administratively on Whitney's behalf. I already knew Laurie was behind, because I too had sent her several requests for comment by Whitney on a given topic, and all had remained unanswered. There were reports that Laurie had failed to send thank-you notes to those who sent the baby gifts for her birthday, and other basic administrative assistant failures.

John Houston contacted me in a veritable rage, demanding to know why Laurie was ignoring his attempts at contact. He had been inquiring as to the well-being and health of his daughter in anticipation of the forthcoming tour scheduled immediately after the filming concluded.

There was good cause for him to be worried. In reality, Laurie simply was not then, nor had she ever been, qualified to fulfill the role she had been given. She had completely lost the thread. All the faxes and memos I had been forwarding to her regarding the upcoming Brunei tour, all those she had received from John, and all others, had gone unanswered. During one encounter, when she was responding hysterically to me about all of this, she took off her dark glasses, revealing that her eyes looked like piss-holes in the snow, but she insisted that she was not under the influence of any drugs. She was wrecked, and her demeanor on that occasion sadly was likely because she needed desperately to feed her habit.

We had a three-day break from filming, and Whitney was able to spend a relaxing long weekend with the baby at the house. However, when I went to pick her up to leave for the set on Monday, I was told she was indisposed and would not be going to the set that day. And that's when the crap really hit the fan. Big time. Laurie tearfully confided in me that she and others, including Whitney, were totally addicted to their drugs of choice, and that they had something Laurie referred to as an "emotional dependency." I knew then that we were in serious trouble. Laurie readily admitted to me that with the exception of myself, Roberta, Silvia, Wendy, and Aunt Bae, most of the staff present in Arizona that spring spent the best part of the film venture snorting cocaine and smoking marijuana.

I inquired as to where they were getting their drugs, and she told me it was Quietfire. After confirming the story, I physically cornered Quietfire, leaving him in no doubt that if he did not immediately cease to supply our party in general, and stop helping Whitney in particular to destroy herself with his poison, his continued tenure on the planet was to be extremely short-lived.

Quietfire appeared mortified by my allegations, and the venom associated with my threats to annihilate him forthwith scared the crap out of him. He openly admitted that in the past he had indeed supplied substances for the group, but that was a historical event and, for the duration of this film project, he had been at pains to avoid any potential of being asked to provide the drugs, keeping his distance socially when not actually engaged in applying makeup to Whitney's face.

In fairness to Quietfire, he had indeed kept to himself on this project, spending more time with the masseuse than our usual crew, and that factor favored his denial, saving his good looks and general well-being. It was very soon thereafter revealed and confirmed that he was not the supplier of our group at this time.

It turned out that Anita Baxter, the outside vendor who was one of Whitney's New Jersey friends, had shown up to stay at the luxury Camelback Inn Resort & Spa that weekend along with a sidekick. Whitney visited them there covertly and remained for thirty-six hours, reportedly without the knowledge of her house support staff and personnel, none of whom had contacted me. Far from spending a relaxing weekend with the baby at the house, she had been with Anita at the hotel, partying and snorting the poison up her nose the entire time. During that dreadful period, others had reportedly visited Anita's room to acquire their supplies, without knowing that Whitney was hiding in the wardrobe, where she remained for the duration of their drug deal.

I was especially disappointed when I found out that Carol Ensminger had succumbed to the drug-imbibing insanity that had taken over our group. Knowing that she had fought against and beaten the ravages of heroin addiction, I felt so sorry for her. I also knew she was under incredible pressure following the recent death of her husband. Even so, Carol kept to herself and did what she had to do behind closed doors and in private. My immediate fear was that perhaps Roberta Quick, the baby's security, was also involved, but I need not have worried—Roberta was as clean as a whistle. She and I discussed what was happening around us, and she was similarly astounded by the depth of the problem.

Whitney overdosed that weekend. I was not allowed to see her but learned that she was nearly unconscious, unable to walk, talk, or even sit up in bed. She could not be taken to a hospital, nor could a doctor be called to the hotel room where she remained because of the media scandal that would have ensued. She was kept in the hotel and tended to there. Our world was falling apart around us. Whitney's shoots were canceled for the week, affecting the entire itinerary and other actors, with no guessing as to what the cost must have been. Forest Whitaker was mortified at the need to alter all the filming, knocking all plans haywire. I felt sorry for him and embarrassed from the perspective of our team. My interaction with the crew from that point on was increasingly apologetic.

As the official version of Whitney's nonappearance on set was throat and voice related, Dr. Julian Groff, Whitney's ENT physician, was flown in from Florida. In fairness, his presence was necessary, as it was true that she could not speak. Her voice box had completely seized up. After examining her, he confirmed that she had overdosed. He gave me his prognosis on her voice as we glided through the Grand Canyon. She simply could not carry on like this. In a nutshell, he told me that unless Whitney stopped taking drugs that affected her throat and also had an operation to clear the damage occasioned thus far, within eight months the injury to her vocal chords could become permanent and she would never again be able to sing. Whitney would lose her voice. Her gift. He was asking me to facilitate some positive action to protect Whitney from herself and others, placing a heavy load on my shoulders that sunny afternoon.

My anger and actual hatred toward all those who had facilitated Whitney's ability to do this to herself was profound. Clive Davis and the Arista machine, promoters and producers who lived off her fame, everyone at Nippy Inc., her staff. Everyone. The burning ire I felt was broad and deep. So many wanted only to take from a person so giving, without considering or caring whatsoever about how it was affecting her. Something began to brew within me. I could sense an inevitability approaching. I would have to do something, no matter what it meant for me personally.

In hindsight, it's obvious that Aunt Bae knew all about the narcotics-induced breakdown. But she didn't have the wherewithal to rein in Whitney or her crew. She could scold them, and she did, but what they all desperately needed was to go into rehab. She saw how angry and upset the turn of events had made me and she took me aside. She told me she knew how much I cared for Whitney's well-being and tearfully begged me not to lose heart. I believed that she did not want me to give up and was relying on me to somehow sort this mess out.

"If by taking Whitney's hand I could transfer all of her problems onto my shoulders, I would grasp it and never let go, to relieve her of her burdens," I confided in Bae. Her response completely blind-sided me.

"David, you're too good to be White. You're just too good to be White, you know that?"

I wondered what that meant. Only Aunt Bae would be able to answer the question, and at that moment my mind was elsewhere. I was carrying the weight of the world and felt like a man very much alone. Plus, I felt like a failure. How had I let my principal slip away from me for thirty-six hours so she could hide in a wardrobe and binge on coke? She'd devised a complex plan to do so, and it forced me to face the truth: if things continued as is, everything would crash and burn. I took no solace in the realization that I could guard her against nearly all external threats but couldn't save her from the threat she posed to herself. How long had she been like this? I'd attributed the previous no-shows and meltdowns to Bobby's negative influence, but how much had drugs played their part regardless of him? Was he the cause or simply a facilitator? I just didn't know.

15

No Regrets

The filming of *Waiting to Exhale* came to an end with the words "It's a wrap" late one night on the edge of a lake outside Phoenix. But Whitney would have to return after the Brunei tour to complete a shoot that had been postponed due to the week of enforced standdown. As the entourage returned to New Jersey to prepare for the tour, Whitney made a quick trip to Florida so Dr. Groff could work his temporary magic.

We all had high hopes that the short Brunei-Singapore tour would be a much-needed tonic for the recent ills befalling the family. However, I obviously had good cause for serious concern. My combined angst and disappointment over the group drug addiction situation could not have been more acute.

I had researched and was patently aware of the attitude of Singapore authorities to drug use in their country. Penalties for being in possession of illegal substances were severe and among the most punitive in the world. Importation and supply of such substances carried a maximum penalty of the death sentence, which was reportedly carried out within forty-eight hours of conviction in certain circumstances. So I was deeply concerned, as addiction is not something one can simply switch on and off at will. Knowing the tactics that had been used for smuggling in the past, and the probability that need for drugs would overrule any common sense, the scene was set for disaster.

Following a week of rehearsals at BKB Studios in New Jersey—so named in honor of Bobbi Kristina—we flew to Brunei on April 22. The sultan of the tiny nation nestled on the northern coast of the island of Borneo had commissioned two shows for his princess niece's eighteenth birthday. Whitney was her gift. The cost for the sultan was in the millions, but a mere trifle for the coming-of-age birthday of the young princess.

The entire group was excited about going to Brunei, as it was rumored that all tour personnel would be the recipients of handsome and excessively generous gifts of many thousands of dollars each. On arrival, however, we learned that this was not to be, due to the abhorrent behavior of our immediate predecessors, the tour staff of Michael Jackson. It was alleged that the out-of-control bunch had seriously trashed a hotel there and, in consequence, any such gifts were voided for the future. The news somewhat subdued the group's enthusiasm.

Despite this, we were truly well received and accommodated upon arrival, with Whitney being given one of the sultan's mansions for her stay. It appeared every child of the family had their own staffed mansion, with the son possessing a number of properties, including a warehouse the size of an aircraft hangar full of the most exotic cars in existence, and another full of Formula One racing cars. For these there was a professional racecourse built within the grounds of the sprawling palace. There was yet another structure full of Rolls-Royce and Bentley vehicles, and so it went, on and on.

I had never seen accumulated wealth that compared with that of the sultan of Brunei (even in the Saudi and other Middle Eastern protection details I had been on). I was most impressed with the collection of firearms, including a gold-covered AK-47 and a number of exquisite diamond-encrusted sidearms, all representative of a coveted collection rather than weapons of choice for regular use, as they were encased in glass and very deliberately on display. I would have loved a few hours on the range with some of them.

The first show on the twenty-fifth, a sort of warm-up for the following night's special for the princess, went off quite well, and all breathed a sigh of relief—Dr. Groff's magic had worked. The show was equally as good as our last shows in South Africa some four months prior. The next morning I went to check on the mansion. To my utter horror, there on the table in the hallway was an ashtray containing three well-smoked roaches. Holy crap! They had done it. They had imported dope into Brunei. I grabbed the joints from the ashtray and stuffed them into my pocket, later disposing of them down a toilet back at the hotel, hoping none of the mansion cleaning staff had seen, or if they had, didn't know what they were.

Of course, and as usual, no one could look me in the eye. In my naïveté, or perhaps an ever-present hope against hope, it never occurred to me that other substances may also have been introduced into the country by the same means I had learned of from Carol those many months ago. In fairness, the evidence I had found could well have belonged to just Laurie, and not to other members of the group. I did not know, nor did I challenge. If it helped Laurie keep it together, that would be fine by me. After Phoenix, it remained patently obvious she was not operating on all cylinders and needed professional help. She was no longer an asset but a liability to Whitney, the tour, and herself.

That night, to my horror, Whitney's voice faltered and failed during the first song. She forced herself to complete it, relying on the dreadful scratchy and squeaky noise emanating from her. She tried to speak to explain what had happened to the audience, and all that came out was a hoarse whisper, a croak of undecipherable sounds. To my eternal embarrassment and escalating anger, Whitney continued with the show.

I caught Laurie's eye in the audience and could tell that she saw my anger. I sought her out, but she had vanished. Toni Chambers feigned a valiant demonstration of support in the wings, clapping and cheering mindlessly, but for me it came across as being shallow and inappropriate. Whitney struggled through to a bitter, sorry, and long overdue end to the most humiliating and saddest show I had ever witnessed. Dr. Groff's predictions were coming to pass, his professional timing impeccable.

I was possessed by unspeakable anger. I resolved there and then that I would never again sit through another pitiful display like that one. I would now pursue with a vengeance what Dr. Groff had demanded of me weeks earlier as we soared in the Cessna. I would do something about it.

As I've said before, when I become angry, I am not a nice person to deal with. I steeled myself mentally for what would be a frustrating and futile course of action for me. But I felt obligated to do it. I approached Toni Chambers, now seemingly promoted above and beyond John Houston's authority in the corporation, and pointedly stated that Whitney needed help. To my astonishment and disgust, Toni, ironically supported by Laurie Badami, refused to provide any assistance to Whitney. She stated categorically that she would not consider any treatment or rehabilitation for her, as to do so, by her reasoning, would damage Whitney's reputation and career.

Holy God!

What was she saying?

What the hell was I listening to?

Unbelievable!

The executives were more concerned with her image, her global reputation, and her ability to make money and honor her contracts (and their own exorbitant salaries) than they were with helping Whitney with her problem, despite the fact that it had clearly left her with no voice with which to sing.

I was gobsmacked. I did not expect such selfish ruthlessness. The absence of care, compassion, empathy, or even understanding was inexplicable to me. Their stance regarding the destruction of Whitney's reputation for admitting to such a problem did not hold water with me. Many high-profile personalities, such as members of the timeless rock group Aerosmith, as just one example, openly and publicly admitted their drug abuse and the effect it had on them. Those stars moved to redress their addictions, and succeeded, improving their reputations in the process, naturally and deservedly so. Toni's argument was as hollow as it was reckless, and undoubtedly dangerous.

Exasperated, I went to Whitney's personal attorney, Sheldon Platt, who was traveling with us at the time. He listened carefully—as he always did—and advised me to contact attorney Tom Weisenbeck on our return to the United States. Toni had independently told me to do the same. So this was the way this matter was to be handled. It was as if the disastrous show had never happened, Whitney did not have an ongoing problem, and all was well in their money-earning empire.

While they pretended their advice to approach the outside attorney was given with the purpose of helping Whitney, it was obvious to me that both Sheldon and Toni did this for selfish reasons. It was clearly an effort to distance themselves from direct knowledge. They were fashioning their future plea: *I had no idea at all, no knowledge whatsoever.* Planning for plausible deniability.

It was also a way to find out through a third-party lawyer precisely what I knew and to what extent I could now be deemed a threat. Toni was not very skillful in hiding this strategy from me—she told me straight out that through my speaking with Tom she could "learn the extent of my knowledge." There was no statement in there that sounded remotely like, "so we can assess and translate that into action for the betterment of Whitney and her health." No. They wanted to know what I knew so they could move to hide, deny, and obfuscate should the truth come to light and threaten to compromise them as individuals.

The writing was clearly on the wall for me. I could go along with the farce that everything was fine, and perhaps keep my job if it wasn't already too late. Or I could persist in my attempts to reach someone who would try to help Whitney, and in that pursuit, most likely gain nothing more than my own loss of employment. But I felt passionately that it was my professional duty to pursue this for Whitney's benefit and her well-being, even if she resisted, and regardless of what it might mean for me personally. Further, to continue to work for her would mean to continue to stand by and witness her suffering and self-destruction. I didn't want that. I couldn't do that.

I knew I stood alone, at odds with those I was targeting and those who held positions of power. I had stood alone before, and I have done so since. It was not a place unfamiliar to me, nor one I feared. The one issue they knew they had was that I was a police officer, a collator of information who commits everything to writing, creating paper trails, and that will always be a problem for those who lie or hide behind denial tactics.

In this case, however, I had never personally seen Whitney use any drug beyond nicotine and alcohol. There were no photographs and no audio recordings. I had only secondhand accounts from people who would probably recant, refuting what I recorded in my notes. But I had my integrity as a professional whose motive was not tainted by self-advancement. I was prepared to sacrifice myself as the metaphorical bullet catcher. I would not be denied my attempt to do right by Whitney.

On arrival in Singapore, we proceeded to the Sheraton Hotel, where a strange moment occurred that illustrated to me the disenfranchisement of John Houston from the main fold of players. We were at the hotel pool. I sat with John on one side, while Cissy, Toni, and the rest sat on the other. Judging by strange glances back and forth, and a general vibe in the air, it was clear to me that John was not part of the movers-and-shakers group anymore. Michael Houston moved back and forth between his father's group and his mother's.

Clearly something was happening at that level, and it did not bode well for me. John's control was being usurped by the ladies, and Toni Chambers was being anointed queen. The natural presumption was that it was with Whitney's complete acquiescence and support. It was sad for me to see. I saw John as the glue that held this ever-disintegrating and dysfunctional band together. John shared my concerns for Whitney's health and well-being, but he seemed powerless, or was perhaps otherwise engaged in battles of his own.

The show in Singapore, only a few days after the Brunei debacle, was maybe one of the best I had ever heard Whitney perform. To me it was reminiscent of her concert for the troops returning from Operation Desert Storm in 1991. She'd done it again. Did this mean there was no need to worry myself about her health? If she could pull this level of performance out of a hat, then clearly what happened in Brunei was a one-off, having no real consequence. Of course, that wasn't the case. But this glimmer of normalcy was enough for the executives to cling to in support of their unwillingness to help her.

Another thing the executives latched onto was the fact that, beyond cutting a couple of songs for the *Waiting to Exhale* soundtrack and a final filming session to capture what had been lost when Whitney overdosed in Arizona, there were no other performances scheduled for the foreseeable future. There appeared to lie ahead a good stretch of time to rest, perhaps seek the much-needed participation of Dr. Groff, and generally recuperate from the physical and emotional exhaustion that had become her norm since the success of *The Bodyguard*.

We returned to the United States on April 30, 1995, and by May 3 I had completed my report and sent it to Tom Weisenbeck, as requested. In it I detailed everything I had learned in Arizona and what had happened since. I wrote of my duty to protect my principal from harm. I expressed my opinion that the harm she was receiving at her own hand, encouraged and enabled by the majority of those in her entourage, was one that I was not qualified to address other than to bring it to the attention of those who could.

I relayed what Dr. Groff had told me as we flew through America's deep red gorge. I explained how Whitney's voice was in danger. Everyone knew Whitney's voice was everything. If they didn't care about her as a person, about the fact that she was clearly unhappy, suffering and enduring pain, at least they would want to do something to protect that golden voice. That was my thought.

I knew also that Whitney's voice was her own salvation. Not because of the money it earned her, but because it was her soul and her spirit. Singing was her medicine. It was her escape, her strength, her prayer, and her fun as well. It was everything to her. It was a gift she received, perfected through hard work, and turned around and gave back to the world. I so hoped that the powers that be would heed the warning I penned in my report. Not for myself, my pride, or my need to be right. For Whitney. She deserved help from all those whom she had helped. It was her turn to receive. Our turn to give back. It had been so long since I had seen the joyful, fun-loving girl I rode a roller coaster with in Copenhagen. That wide grin, those sparkling eyes, that infectious laugh. I knew she was in there, and I felt helpless to find her.

A period of inactivity lay ahead, at least in comparison with our usual hectic schedule. There was plenty to do at the estate and office, of course, but as the heat of summer started to give way to autumn, I had some downtime. I decided to apply some preservative to the wood roof tiles that covered the farmhouse I had bought in Fredon, New Jersey. As I climbed up the ladder, it slipped from under me and off I tumbled, landing in the driveway, extending an arm to break my fall. The result: my left wrist was forced to meet my left elbow, shattering all the bones in the forearm in the process.

I was alone on the property at the time, and after jumping around the driveway believing my pager had become embedded inside my hip, I wrapped my shortened left arm in a wet tea towel and drove to the hospital in Newton, locally known as "Newton Mutant Hospital" for reasons I was about to discover. I approached the desk and asked for assistance. The receptionist told me I would have to fill out paperwork, present my insurance (US medical care is a very profitable business), and wait my turn. It was a rote recitation, and she didn't look up or take a breath as she thrust a prepared clipboard full of forms at me.

I pulled the towel off my smashed arm and felt the blood finally draining from my head as dizziness took over. The receptionist's eyes bugged out of her head, and she immediately started calling for an emergency crew as I slowly slipped to the floor, clipboard not in hand.

I came to in an operating room with someone purporting to be a doctor at my side. To my mind he had altogether too much acne to be credibly old enough to be a physician, but there he was, musing over my damaged lower left arm. A nurse was preparing to put in a catheter, which I promptly refused. My luckless doctor was talking about an operation to re-extend the forearm and sort out what appeared to be twice as many bones in the wrist area than should have been there. To do so he intended to insert metal rods and some form of external apparatus for stability. I just wanted a plaster cast and the usual six weeks of scratching with a knitting needle until the damned thing was cut off. Yes, I have broken a few bones in my time. But this doctor had something else in mind, so I simply told him to get on with whatever it was. I needed full use of my arm as soon as possible. They put me to sleep.

I awoke from the surgery with a metal bar sticking out of my hand and another in the middle of my forearm, with an identical metal bar holding them apart and rigid. That was how it remained, covered in bandages, for the next six weeks. I had to clean the wounds with peroxide daily to stop infection in the exposed open wounds giving access to the bones underneath.

When I went in for the reverse operation to remove the metal splints, the anesthetist accidentally dislocated my jaw as he woke me from the operation, apparently while removing some tube they had stuffed down my throat. I was left floundering and unable to breathe in consequence, as my windpipe was being depressed by the relocating of my jaw. The nurses and doctors ran around looking for a specialist to untangle whatever they had done, seemingly an unprecedented event for them.

I decided I could not wait for the Newton Mutants to get their act together, and so, effectively, saved myself. To the wide-eyed amazement of the staff left to watch me dying, I reached up and manipulated my own jaw into the sockets from which they had forcibly and unceremoniously been removed. At that moment some form of bone specialist in a white coat dashed into the postoperative room. Too little, too late.

For months thereafter my jaw clicked every time I opened and closed my mouth. The resetting of my lower arm and wrist was also not done properly. Granted, they had more bone dust than bones to play with and manipulate into place, but their attempts had effectively crippled the wrist and left it with only 10 percent elevation and rotational capability. Further, the bones protruded against overly taut skin like marbles in a balloon, resulting in the most god-awful looking wrist I had ever seen still affixed to an arm. I was sent to a specialist who told me he could either remove bone from my hip or use cadaver bone and get me up to a possible 80 percent rotational and bending capability. I wasn't keen on either option, and the price was astronomical. Being right-hand dominant, I chose to let it be.

In the immediate aftermath of the fall and initial surgery, when I was still not healed enough to work, Whitney and Bobby went on a late summer holiday to a Mexican resort and took Tom LeBrun with them. Tom had joined our security team for the South Africa trip. Certainly, a strange option when Big Bob would have been my natural choice for team leadership. Tom was a relative newcomer to the fold with limited experience and issues with the carriage of firearms. I learned later that Tom didn't last long, as it was Bobby's opinion that he had fallen in love with Whitney and, of course, had to go.

In early October, I was called to a meeting at the offices of Tom Weisenbeck in Florham Park. I knew then that the end was nigh. I suited up and duly attended, with a tape recorder in my briefcase. I liked Tom a lot. We had been through much together in the past few years and had developed a sincere and earnest personal friendship as well as a great working rapport, and I felt sorry that he had been placed in that position. I allowed Tom to do the talking without interruption. It was very uncomfortable for him. My silence was perhaps unexpected, as I was never known for my lack of vocal contributions to any conversation, and I believe I made him wish he had not been assigned this task. I was trying to make it as painless as possible for him.

The story was that everyone was extremely grateful for my report, and for my care and concern for my principal and her family and associates. In response to the report, it had been decided that Whitney was to curtail her touring activities, and a professional with international expertise was no longer needed to protect her. She was reportedly intending to limit her performances to the United States in the foreseeable future.

I was assured, should she ever decide to travel abroad in the future, they would call on me without hesitation. We both knew that was said only as a meaningless formality. I was thanked for my service, and October 31, 1995, was my agreed-on termination date. I told Tom that I required something for my service, loyalty, and dedication over the years. I suspected this was the moment he held his breath, not knowing what the hell I was going to demand. I said I wished simply for signed letters of recommendation from him, Sheldon Platt, and John Houston, to use if and when I were offered a position for someone I deemed worthy of dying for. That was all I was asking? Oh, simple as that? Perfect! Instantaneous agreement.

All that remained was an arrangement to return radios, a cell phone, and other company equipment I had, and that would be a satisfactory conclusion to what had been a seven-and-a-half-year relationship looking after the most significant entertainer of the time, the veritable and indisputable Queen of Pop, and a person generally loved by all who had encountered her or listened to her music. I never saw Whitney again.

As the years have passed, there have been many developments in my life, both good and bad. But perhaps the saddest of all was the dreadful and unbelievable shock delivered by Fox News on the afternoon of February 11, 2012. I was sitting in front of my computer, typing surveillance reports, the TV on and to my left, the vast and gleaming expanse of the Atlantic Ocean to my right. At this point I had relocated to Florida with an office on the thirty-fourth floor. As the announcer spoke, I felt like he was delivering a bullet to my heart: Whitney Houston was dead. Before the end of the broadcast, the telephone started ringing. Media outlets the world over. With her body still warm, they wanted their pound of flesh.

For days, I refused to answer the telephone, needing time for grieving on my own. Whitney's death by drowning was determined to be accidental. But was it really? Accidents can be avoided with some proper planning and advised intervention, can't they? Who could not see this "accident" coming? Who contributed to it?

Isolating specific names is no longer important. They all know who they are. On hearing this terrible news, I experienced a wave of anger that brought me straight back to what had overwhelmed me at the end of the filming of *Waiting to Exhale*. It was similar to the way a scent can trigger a vivid memory and lived sensation, no matter how many years have passed. To my mind, everyone—and I mean everyone without exception—family, friends, advisers—was to blame. Some did try to a greater or lesser extent, all subject only to what their given positions allowed for. Many did nothing at all. Many looked the other way. Many pretended. And many encouraged and enabled.

My anger was reignited some three years later when on January 31, 2015, Bobbi Kristina succumbed to an identical fate for similar reasons. When I had last seen her, she was an adorable baby running around the hotel corridor, darting in and out of my room shouting "oh-oh!" *Oh-oh, indeed, Bobbi Kristina.* Such a painful tragedy. Beautiful people removed from this world, largely through circumstances of their own making but with more than ample contribution and negligence on the parts of many.

The anger I carry over these senseless deaths is one that has not gone away even after all these years. Even after writing this book in an attempt to come to terms with it, I don't think it ever will.

Epilogue

To my mind, "I Will Always Love You" was my boss's finest song. Whitney's parting song to her film bodyguard, Frank Farmer, who technically served her well, failing only in the human emotions department. And so, for reasons not understandable to many, I suspect, they parted company. I have looked at the lyrics to that song often and, in preparing a fitting conclusion to this book, I experienced what for me was an epiphany of sorts. After all these years.

Consider the story I've just told, and then reverse the direction of the lyrics. Sung not from the protectee to the protector, but the other way around. From me to her.

The first lines are about staying, only to be in the way.

I ultimately acted in an attempt to protect my principal from herself. I *did* want to get in her way. Although there was some mock appreciation for what I sought to achieve, the reality was that I had thrown myself under the bus on her behalf. No one remaining could look me in the eye. My presence made them very uncomfortable. So to stay would only put me in their way, the way of those who bear that shame and guilt. Those who controlled her.

In the song's next lines, the singer says he'll go, but will think of her every step of the way.

It was the right thing to do. I had to go. They knew it. I knew it. And most important, Whitney knew it too. Maybe not through any thought processing and deduction of her own, but certainly through the pressure of self-serving advisers and "friends." Would any of that nonsense stop me from thinking of her? Of course not. The time we spent together, the laughter we shared, the challenges we tackled, the unspoken language we developed, the conversations we had—she will always be with me. I have indeed thought of her every step of the way. Here we are now, a quarter of a century later, and the wounds are as fresh as when first inflicted, my anger dissipating only slightly from the catharsis of penning this story.

The next verse starts by talking of bittersweet memories.

My story is full of truly bittersweet memories, and it is undoubtedly I who took them with me. I feel certain that Whitney would never have had the time nor inclination to give any such second thought to our professional relationship. I really was not that important to her at the end of the day. But perhaps, just perhaps, through the love, care, and fear in the eyes of Aunt Bae, Whitney may have had cause to fleetingly reflect upon and remember the British bodyguard who had been willing to sacrifice his life for hers.

The following lines are the goodbye and don't cry. He's not what she needs.

As explained previously, there was no actual goodbye from Whitney, or from me—not the spoken word, not the written word, not even a small handwritten note stuck under a door. So no tears—not from her, anyway. Neither the environment nor personalities involved allowed for goodbyes. When you were no longer in sight, you didn't exist. You were gone, forgotten. It was easier that way. Less embarrassing. No one to push the guilt buttons, which is definitively and definitely what Whitney did not want or need—something that would render her life more difficult to bear than it already was. So it was obvious, yet unspoken between us. We no longer needed each other.

The next verse wishes her a life of kindness, fulfilled dreams, joy, and above all, love.

Yes, I truly wished life would treat Whitney kindly. It was essentially the impossible dream for her, but hope springs eternal even against all the odds. She was always battling those odds—and losing more often than not. There would be no more children, no house in Colorado. The selection of Atlanta as a second home was a very poor substitute, and her home in New Jersey was ultimately lost to a sheriff's sale for a host of financially debilitating reasons.

She still had so much to offer the world. But my hopes for her to have all she dreamed of could never materialize as long as she remained so tormented, be it by the abuse of others, her dependency on narcotics, or her misplaced loyalties. The world at large, and I in particular, wished for her all the joy and happiness possible. We owed it to her, after what she had given us.

In reality, I doubt she ever experienced what was deservedly hers. It is true—above all else, I wished her the love she so desperately sought. But I suspect Whitney never truly found that either, and there was no real peace for her, only the elusive pursuit of happiness. What a damned waste.

Rest in peace, boss.

It is now and will always be my eternal hope that you may finally spend some quality time with your father and daughter, far from those who could and should have done something to help, but didn't.

I Will Always Love You, Boss.

Acknowledgments

Thanks to all those whose love and support has guided, assisted, and inspired me in so many ways through the cathartic process of writing this book, especially my Peruvian princess Toti, my daughter Sara, her husband Russ, and my grandsons Jac and Tomas.

I would also like to acknowledge the insight, guidance, and encouragement of my agent, Mark Falkin, and the team at Chicago Review Press headed by Jerome Pohlen, in particular Devon Freeny and his experts, whose unsurpassed knowledge and sense of justice helped create this final product.